Nine Lives Plus One

Nine Lives Plus One

an incredible story of
surviving and living

SD WEBSTER

Copyright © 2014 by SD Webster.

Library and Archives Canada Cataloguing in Publication

Webster, S.D., 1968-, author
   Nine Lives Plus One: an incredible story of surviving
   and living/SD Webster.

ISBN 978-0-9936496-2-2 (pbk.)

1. Webster, S. D., 1968.

2. Cancer—Patients—Canada—Biography.

3. Cancer—Psychological aspects.

I. Title. II. Title: 9 lives plus 1.

Editing by Manley Mann Media
Cover and text design by Gunay Kelly
Typeset in Adobe Caslon Pro and Gill Sans

First Edition
Printed and bound in the United States of America
Available from Amazon.com and other online stores

10 9 8 7 6 5 4 3 2 1

This book is dedicated to Kelsey and Sam.
I love you now and forever.

ACKNOWLEDGEMENTS

This book has evolved over many years; sometimes written in desperation to have my experience captured so I could be part of the world's memory (or at least memories of those in my small circle of the world). It started out as a book of poems or songs. I managed to work my way from verses and stanzas to paragraphs after awhile. The paragraphs became pages after almost seven years of a "normal," peaceful life had an abrupt near ending. I then cobbled together nearly a hundred pages of stories leading from one tragedy and triumph to another.

Writing a book was a safety net I had threatened to jump into all my life. The dream of that book—this book— was taken away by my health, so I had to cross the falls by finding my own balance.

One night, I was at a family party, telling everyone about my book. I joked about being on Oprah with my tale of surviving almost everything. My aunt Marilyn suggested I call the book "Nine Lives Plus One" and that I get a ghostwriter to give me the proper perspective. In a sense, she called my bluff.

Fate led me to Jaime Mann, my kindred spirit who had the inevitable job of entering my mind for brief visits to put more eloquence and structure into my written life, and Christine Gordon Manley, our editor, who paid the real price by trying to bring order to the pile of words.

There are many people who, without their support, this book would not have been possible.

My biological family—my blood family—who have always stood by me. Especially my mother, Debbie, who showed me where I got all of my special gifts and what courage really means.

My brother Scot and his wife, Deborah, who took me into their lives and loved me unconditionally. I think of how far we have come in seventeen years, and it brings a smile to my face.

Doug, Jackie, Ross, and Sandra. All my aunts, uncles, and cousins: I love you and I thank you for being part of my journey.

John and Heather. My in-laws, who have flown more rescue missions to save Sandra, Sam, and I than I can count. Your grace has granted us grace.

My survival depended on finding the right people at the right time with the right treatments. The ones who stand out to me most, because of their kindness and compassion for wretch-like me, are Dr. Wynham Wilson, Dr. Darrell White, Dr. George Carruthers, and Dr. Augustus Grant. I am also thankful to, and for, nurses Pia Nierman and Laura Cormier, along with all of their colleagues.

I am grateful to have many friends and families over the years help me, and I am truly a better person because of all of you. You have given me hope and taught me many life lessons with your actions. You have been around me through all life's ups and downs as I have been there for them.

Bobby and Sue Lapierre. Bobby and I have known each other for the past fifteen years, and we're like two peas in a pod...an old married couple (we joke that we are heterosexual life partners). Susan, whom I have known just as long, is loving, caring, and compassionate; she is everything Bobby needs (and I have borrowed from her when not around my own wife). My god, she is a good person. Both of our wives make up for the shit we cause.

Neil Williams. The person I have known the longest on this earth besides my family. How fortunate I have been to have such a loyal friend who has always been loving, kind, and courageous since I first saw his face in the backyard.

Kevin Webster. My brother in all senses of what that word means, we have been together for over 44 years—through thick and thin. I can't think of a better man to sit in a foxhole with. Kevin, you are always in my heart brother, forever and ever.

Mom and Dad (Don and Barb). I have been the prodigal son, and you have done everything parents could do for, and given everything parents could give to, a child. I was brought to angels by God and have been taught by the best on how to live and thrive in this world. My love for you is eternal.

Sam and Kelsey. I wrote this book really for you. As a testimony to how hard I tried to stay on this earth to be with you. I look at you, touch you, and think how I would like to turn into particles and fly into you to make us together as one, but I guess that is the thing: We are as one and I will always be part of you. I am the proudest when I look at my two miracles.

Sandra. My better half. Blessed is the day I met you. Never did I think that anyone would be able to capture my heart. You not only captured it, but you control it. You are my hero, my calmness, and my partner in every sense. The journey has been long, but we always had fun and took care of each other. I love you, always and forever.

Secret Prayer

Eternal it springs

Around the corner it lingers
Inside the very core of your being
Interlocking everything

Desperate to find it
Hope to be able to see
Desperate without it
Hope comes back to me

Hope is life's sweetest song
God, Hum a bit for me
Help me sing along

Hope is life's sweetest song
God, Hum a bit for me
Help me sing along

Hope is life's sweetest song
God, Hum a bit for me
Help me sing along

When someone in a white coat sits you down and tells you that you have Stage IV cancer, a lot happens in your head.

You realize you have no more time for dreams.
Time takes on new meaning.
You imagine how you want your funeral to look.
Inside your head, you die a thousand times.

After awhile, you learn how to block it out. You take the darkness, put it in a box, and store it on a shelf somewhere in the back of your mind.

When someone in a white coat sits you down and tells you that you have cancer after you thought you'd beaten it five years earlier, the same thoughts go through your head, except it also feels like you're on the ice playing hockey and you dodge a big hit only to get smoked into the boards the second you turn around.

It knocks the wind out of you.

How can you be having this conversation with a doctor again?

It wasn't supposed to come back…

Your life becomes part fiction that you believe and part non-fiction that you don't reveal.

This is the story of my battle with cancer. So far I'm winning, but it's given me the ass kicking of a lifetime.

This is not a story of self-pity. It's the story of a warrior at constant battle.

Cancer has gotten in more than a few good blows.

Do I wish I could rewrite my history and leave out the whole fighting for my life on a daily basis bit? Of course I do. But I can't.

I'll never be able to have a better past, but I am going to share the steps I took—the good ones and the bad ones—to try to have a better future, a future I thought I would never have.

This isn't a flowery feel-good tale about surviving cancer. This is my account of how this ugly disease and its equally-as-ugly treatment have ravaged my mind and body, leaving me with more scars than I can count.

In 1987, I started fighting for my life. The details are foggy in some parts. Had I known back then what I was in for, I would have kept better notes. But life doesn't work like that, does it?

With the help of my parents, my brother, my friends, and my wife, I have pieced together this recollection.

Since the time I was nineteen, cancer has reared its ugly head four times. I was an addict by the time I was twenty. My first wife and I separated shortly after bringing a beautiful baby girl into the world when I was twenty-five. I got sober when I was twenty-seven. I lost my best friend to gambling the year after.

Fighting cancer has almost killed me. The chemo literally broke my heart. But I continue to fight. I've found love and life again. I even fathered another child, despite being told I never would. And I have never gone back to the bottle.

This book does not take a familiar form, but then again, neither do I. A book about my life wouldn't be right if it was conventional. I've decided to tell my story through a series of themes that have shaped my life between 1987 and now.

I use Cancer as a character or a voice inside my head, as the bastard that is always there. Sometimes he (I think of him as a he with like a James Earl Jones-like voice) is whispering, sometimes screaming, but he is ever present.

If you're reading this to help you cope with your own cancer, I hope you take comfort in my story and that it encourages you to fight with everything you have because you can beat it. Hope is the greatest weapon you have.

If you have someone in your life battling cancer, they might never tell you the truth about how hard it really is. I hope this story helps you understand what they're going through and they understand how important you are to the fight.

If you're battling addiction, let my story show you that you can keep your demons at bay and the rewards sobriety will give you will be greater then you could have ever dreamed.

To my family, please know that I've always fought as hard as I could, and I will continue to fight because I don't want to leave you. All I really want is for the last thing I see to be you and for that to stay with me when I rejoin the divine.

The Quitter

When you're lost in the Wild, and you're scared as a child,
        And Death looks you bang in the eye,
And you're sore as a boil, it's according to Hoyle
        To cock your revolver and...die.
But the Code of a Man says: "Fight all you can,"
        And self-dissolution is barred.
In hunger and woe, oh, it's easy to blow...
        It's the hell-served-for-breakfast that's hard.

"You're sick of the game!" Well, now that's a shame.
        You're young and you're brave and you're bright.
"You've had a raw deal!" I know—but don't squeal,
        Buck up, do your damnedest, and fight.
It's the plugging away that will win you the day,
        So don't be a piker, old pard!
Just draw on your grit, it's so easy to quit.
        It's the keeping-your-chin-up that's hard.

It's easy to cry that you're beaten—and die;
        It's easy to crawfish and crawl;
But to fight and to fight when hope's out of sight—
        Why that's the best game of them all!
And though you come out of each grueling bout,
        All broken and battered and scarred,
Just have one more try—it's dead easy to die,
        It's the keeping-on-living that's hard.

Robert Service

CONTENTS

PREFACE

My biological grandfather died on the hospital table after having his left mitral valve repaired when he was forty-three. I laid on the very same hospital table almost forty years later with surgeons operating on my left mitral valve.

I have survived so far.

They say I look exactly like him. Maybe he reached back or forward to help me through; maybe it was Sterns Webster or my uncles who died in the Great War. I think it was all of the above and all that were around me now and all yet to come.

Hopefully, I can do the same if I'm needed one day.

I believe we are all connected and that connection leads back to the divine.

45

YEARS IN CANADA

Places I have lived in, run away from, run to, been welcomed in, or kicked out of:

- Halifax, Nova Scotia (4 Times)
- Inverness, Nova Scotia
- Sheet Harbor, Nova Scotia
- Truro, Nova Scotia
- Windsor, Nova Scotia
- Yarmouth, Nova Scotia
- Sydney, Nova Scotia
- Dartmouth, Nova Scotia
- Stanhope, Prince Edward Island (20 summers)
- Charlottetown, Prince Edward Island
- Ottawa, Ontario
- Inuvik, Northwest Territories
- Grande Prairie, Alberta
- St.Albert, Alberta
- Edmonton, Alberta (3 times)
- Kelowna, British Columbia
- Kamloops, British Columbia
- Vancouver, British Columbia

PART ONE
1968–1994

i am as old as the human race. i've been taking lives since before jesus walked the earth and i'll let you in on a little secret. i was headed for his prostate and i would have gotten him before he turned 40 had the whole crucifixion thing not happened. i did get king hezekiah, though. 2 kings 20:6-8. look it up for yourself if you don't believe me.

the egyptians have been writing about me since they first discovered papyrus. of course, they didn't know much about me in those days, but they did write of "abnormal tumors" and "ulcers of the breast." i laughed at their efforts to erase me. brewing up concoctions of pig's ear and barley. prescribing enemas, castor oil, and supposi- tories to get rid of me. using ointments and poultices in the war they were waging against me.

laughable, really. they knew not my strength.

then along came hippocrates. he's the man i have to thank for my name. he was the first to notice a visual dif- ference between benign and malignant tumors. he thought the blood vessels around malignant tumors closely resem- bled the claws of a crab. i didn't do that on purpose, by the way, in case you were wondering. he called me karkinos (greek for crab).

perhaps you've heard of the german translation—der krebs. in poland, i am rak. to the dutch i am kanker. ital- ians know me as cancro. but for the english, french, and even the spaniards, i am cancer.

cancer. humans don't like to say the word. like hold- ing it on their tongues will make me invade them. i am whispered in the dark. never spoken with a smile.

i had it good for a long time. many early physicians have studied me since the days of hippocrates, but i had nothing to worry about until jean astruc and a chemist by the name of bernard came into the picture. i think ofthem as the earliest oncologists. they laid a lot of groundwork for the physicians who would come after them, trying to cut me down at the knees. but i was too great a challenge for them.

in 1761, giovanni morgagni came along. my first true enemy. he learned way too much for my liking. he began doing autopsies on patients, looking for pathological findings.

it all went to hell from there. i haven't been able to hide as easily.

today there are millions of dollars spent every year by hundreds of organizations dedicated to learning how to eradicate me. that really pisses me off. i mean, how would you feel?

i have taken many breasts, lungs, tongues, colons, eyes, bones, livers, and even brains. i do not discriminate. rich, poor, young, old, black, white, english, spanish. i am in the business of killing. blood is all the same.

and there's nothing i like better than a fight.

when i met steven webster, a young kid in great health... strong and athletic... i knew i had to have him. he wouldn't see it coming.

when you're in the line of work that i'm in, you have to get your kicks wherever you can.

C.

1
ADOPTED

I WAS BORN IN HALIFAX in 1968 and, despite several valiant attempts by cancer, my own heart, and addiction, I am not dead yet.

I don't like pain, or the fighting all the time, or the uncertainty. But it has become familiar. It's the price of doing business.

I was adopted at birth. It was a different time and I understand my biological mother's decision. My birth father was non-existent. Drunks are rarely useful. It's really no big drama to me. That's what happened. It is what it is. I'm not mad about it.

She had her reasons. She's a wonderful person, my birth mother, and as hard as that decision was for her to make, I know without a doubt that she made the right choice. We've been in touch over the years and I'm glad to have her in my life.

I have known that I was adopted for as long as I can remember. My parents never tried to hide that fact from me, and I eventually did meet my birth family. I never had any desire to find them, but I was curious, and who knows when I may find myself in need of a bone marrow donor.

I admire and respect my blood family, and I understand and respect the decision they made to give me up. I considered my birth mother a friend. I'm pretty sure I got my absent-mindedness from her and my clumsiness. I also like to think I inherited some of her kind nature and generous spirit, too.

I am also aware that I was the luckiest little son of a bitch in the nursery the day Don and Barb Webster decided they were ready to start a family.

My father is my hero and my mother is one of the greatest blessings in my life.

If there are two other people on the planet as strong in will (Dad) and faith (Mom) as those two, I'd like to meet them. That combination of faith and will makes perfect chemistry for raising someone who would need to know how to survive.

A year after Barb and Don became my Mom and Dad, along came my brother Kevin. Just like that, I had a little brother. Of course, I don't remember much about the acquisition of that little brother, but every memory I have of my childhood includes him. We've been the best of friends for as long as I can remember. He was also adopted and, even though he was always more curious about his birth family than I was, I know he shares my belief that we were two mother-honking lucky little babies.

There is one thing thicker than blood and that is love. Don't let anyone tell you different. My brother and I speak a secret language.

When Kevin was twenty-seven, he decided he needed to meet his biological parents. My mother did the paperwork for both of us, unbeknownst to me. At the time, I was twenty-eight, and trying to sober up and stay employed, so I didn't really care about the fact that Mom gave my biological parents my name.

I ended up getting a letter from the adoption agency with all of the details about my lineage (Scottish/Irish), my birth parents' ages (mother 18, father 19), and vague details about their siblings (mother had 5 sisters, 1 brother; father had a brother and a sister).

Turns out, maybe I did care more about it than I thought I did.

A couple of items fell out of that envelope. There was a picture of me as a baby and some photos of a guy who looked like me in early childhood, playing hockey. And there was a letter:

Dear Steve,

I thought this day would never come. Your full brother Scott is now 25.

What? Wait a second. I had a full brother for twenty-five years? That was an interesting fact. The world is a mysterious place.

I caused my parents so much worry and pain over the years that sometimes I wonder if they knew then what they knew now—that the little baby they brought home from the Guardian Angel home would, as a teenager, be diagnosed with Hodgkin's Disease and would continue to fight cancer and the effects of treatment for his entire adult life—, whether they would have still chosen me.

Then again, I know the answer to that. And I also know what they would say if they heard me talking that way:

Steve, we didn't choose you. You chose us.

From Barb (Steve's Mom)

I remember them saying at the Guardian Angel home that if we weren't happy with the baby, we didn't have to keep him. We could take him back.

I just couldn't believe that.

When I picked Steve up for the first time, that was it. From the first moment, I couldn't imagine not having that child. I couldn't imagine not loving him.

2
ADMIRATION

DAD WAS A pretty important guy in the RCMP, and he was driven to be as successful as possible. In order to do this, he had to continue to move forward in the forces. Anyone who knows anything about the RCMP knows this is code for we moved around a lot when we were growing up.

A lot.

Like, by the time I was ten, we'd lived in ten different places—from Inuvik (for the non-geographically-fluent, that is pretty close to where Santa Claus lives) to Canada's east coast in Cape Breton and pretty much everywhere in between.

Mom worked in administrative roles, but mostly as the administrator of our home. She baked cookies ("cookie crack," as I like to call them) and did all those other motherly things. She is the mother we all dream of. She still makes me chicken noodle soup when I'm sick, for Christ's sake.

Anyway, I have great parents.

I don't consider them or refer to them as my adoptive parents. They're just Mom and Dad. They are my home and I love them.

From Barb

When Steve was little, he was such a funny little guy. He had an imaginary friend who lived in our attic. His name was Frankie Wilson.

One day when Steve was around 3 or 4 years old, he got on the phone and pretended he was calling Frankie.

The conversation went something like this:

"Hi Frankie, this is Steve. How are you? How are the wife and kids?"

Then he would pause for a minute, nod his head.

"Now, when they're bad, what do you do to them?"

Then he would sit there and nod his head, "Uh uh. Uh uh. I see. That's what I'd do to them, too."

He was so content to play on his own. Such an imagination he had! Such a cute little guy.

3
ANCESTRY

I BELIEVE I HAVE my birth father to thank for the alcoholism I have flowing through my blood, but on my adoptive side, I've come from a long line of tough guys.

Yes, my adoptive side, and yes, I'm aware that won't make sense to most of you unless you're adopted, too, and then you'll understand exactly what I mean. Character traits can be inherited from adoptive family members.

Don't believe me? Let me tell you a story about my adoptive grandfather...

It was your average January evening in Charlottetown, as the calendar was just about to change to February 1941. Two policemen, Sterns Webster and Anthony Lund, were doing their regular patrol of the downtown area near King and Pownal Streets when they noticed something wasn't right.

The light was on at the butcher shop and it was the middle of the night.

Lund could see a man standing behind the cash register and he could easily see that it wasn't Peter Trainor, the 78-year-old butcher.

After calling two more policemen for backup, Lund and Webster broke a window to gain entry. In those days, police officers didn't carry guns, so Lund and Webster were unarmed, but they were a couple of pretty tough sons of bitches.

The man they saw standing behind the cash register happened to be Lund's cousin. They wrestled him through a window where he landed in a glass-covered snow bank below and was arrested by one of the backup policemen. In the meantime, a second man was upstairs where the shopkeeper lived. He tried to trick the police by calling them for help. When Webster ran up the stairs, that second man aimed a .32 caliber gun at him and pulled the trigger.

The trigger miraculously stuck, giving Webster enough time to react, wrestle him to the ground, and place him under arrest. (And yes, he probably roughed him up a little more than he had to. At least I like to think he did.)

Both of the apprehended men were covered in blood, as was the massacred body of the butcher, dead after being stabbed twenty-two times by the pair of thugs who had befriended each other in Dorchester Penitentiary.

Sterns Webster was my father's father. He was partially responsible for making the arrest that would lead to the last public hanging in Prince Edward Island.

He and Anthony Lund were both given engraved watches by the family of Peter Trainor as a thank you for the courage they displayed. That watch is one of my father's most prized possessions.

To me, the watch is a reminder of the fucking tough genes that, by blood or not, have helped to shape me into a fighter.

From Don (Steve's Dad)

My father stood 6'4" and he was one tough man. He used to box back in the 1940s, and, at that time, there was a lot of boxing going on around Charlottetown. One day, a fella from the States came into the gym looking for sparring partners.

He asked Dad to go in. This fella told him he knew he wasn't a professional boxer and it wasn't his intent to beat him up. He just needed that long-armed jab of Dad's to help him prepare for the boxing match he had coming up.

So they went ahead and started a sparring match. Dad was doing pretty good with him. Too good I guess, cause this guy started laying it on pretty heavy and hurting him more than he probably should have.

The next round, Dad came in and knocked him out.

That was the end of that.

4
ATHLETE

I WAS AN ATHLETE.

Scratch that "was." I am an athlete.

I might not look the part now, thanks to the fetching waif-like figure cancer has left me with, but in my head I am still the same 200-pound hockey player I was when Hodgkin's came knocking, back in the late 1980s.

When we were kids growing up in cities and towns all across Canada, there was one thing we could always count on: There would be a rink for Kevin and I to pass a puck back and forth on during the winter.

And we were pretty good. Of course, I was a little better than him.

I got a taste for being a star at a very young age. When we were kids living in Inuvik, we were like little mini-Gretzky's, the pair of us. I was the all-time leading scorer in the hockey league up there. I'm not sure if my record has been broken yet, but I like to think not.

Being a jock kept me out of trouble and it gave me a place in the social order of things.

When you play sports, you have an instant connection with a group of like-minded people. Sure, it's surface deep, but guys don't usually need much more than that.

We moved from Inuvik to Dartmouth, Nova Scotia, when I was twelve, and I was pretty much your classic nerd. I'd grown up on Tolkien books, I was in the enrichment class for gifted children, and I liked watching movies from the 1930s and 1940s on CBC.

Being the new kid sucks, but I played hockey, which helped me to fit in pretty quick. Regardless of that, though, I was painfully insecure about my looks and my clothes and all that other adolescent shit.

Dad was Inspector of Intelligence for the RCMP and was responsible for making arrests in the drug trade, but that didn't stop me from finding trouble.

See, in Grade 7 I found a way to be more confident around girls. At my first dance, I had a swig of some "witches brew." If you're not familiar with the concoction, it's a mixture of every type of alcohol from a parent's liquor cabinet poured into one bottle. It tasted horrible, but I immediately loved how it made me feel. The confidence I had was amazing.

By the time I was thirteen years old, I was smoking joints because they were so much easier to get than booze. I don't know if Dad knew or not. I guess I'll find out after he reads this.

At the age of fourteen, I was still playing hockey and running track, but I had gone from being that kid in the gifted class to being the kid with no interest in school whatsoever.

Drinking and smoking up became the norm. I would make up stories to tell my parents ("Some guy stole my glasses") and I would steal money for booze. Or I would just steal the booze.

I had about a fistfight a week. Most were inside a local
traffic rotary circle. I was like a modern gladiator.

From Kevin

Steve was a great brother. Before the drinking started getting out of control, we had a lot of fun together.

In the early 1980s, we lived in Grande Prairie, Alberta. Mom and Dad were out of town and I had a hockey tournament going on. I had gotten a drive home with a team member and his parents. We got home around 10:00 at night, just as a huge party was getting underway.

My friend's parents asked if everything was okay and I said, "oh ya, sure."

I walked into the house and there were people everywhere. There were beer cans all over the place and there were people in my room. There were college kids there and Steve would have been 14 or 15 at the time.

I wasn't too impressed. These people were eating all of the food in the house. There was garbage everywhere. I knew we were going to get in shit for this. When everyone left, I helped Steve clean it up. We threw 5 garbage bags worth of stuff out into a field.

The next morning, everything looked just as it should. I have no idea how we pulled that off, but it was your classic movie scene. Parents away, teenagers throw a party, and hustle all night to cover it up.

Mom and Dad got home and they were in the house for one second before Dad said, "you had a party."

All it took was one crooked picture frame.

Dad was a professional interrogator. You couldn't get away with lying to him. (It also didn't help matters that he was an RCMP officer and they have meetings where they bring up things like noise complaints and parties, and he would have heard that there was a report of one at his own address. We weren't all that wise.)

My limited criminal career came to end when I got caught jokingly robbing some poor kid delivering milk in the school with a modified jackknife. He had Down Syndrome (I was not aware of this) and ran directly to the principal's office.

The lesson here, kids: Nothing good ever comes of sitting in the hallway during class.

Soon after that, when I was in Grade 9, we moved to Grande Prairie, Alberta. I wasn't a nerd anymore. I was a punk who couldn't do algebra. I was a fifteen-year-old hockey player who smoked and drank like a thirty-five year old. Dartmouth ages a guy. I think that was part of the reason for Dad's transfer and the move out west.

It was a good new start. I made a lot of friends that I still have to this day. I played hockey, basketball, and football, and was captain of all teams. I didn't play volleyball because it wasn't violent enough. I had gotten letters from major junior hockey teams, and I played for the local Tier 2 Junior A team at age sixteen.

I would fight anything or anyone.

From Kevin

There was this time in high school when Steve and I were both on the school football team. Now, we went to a high school that had 300 students and the one next door had 1500. You can guess which one had a better pool of talent to choose from. Our squad barely had enough players to make a roster, and so half our offense also played defense.

We did not fare well, but we had a lot of fun. We travelled by bus from Grande Prairie, Alberta, to Dawson Creek, BC, to play a game one weekend and we got stomped.

We were really un-coached. Steve was then the de facto captain of the defense and he had his work cut out for him. After all, some of us were not even fully cognizant of the rules of the game! So a typical huddle went something like this:

"Okay. Everyone come together. We blitz."

We would blitz at least every second play and it was quite a show. For the opposition fans. Anyway, after the game, a bunch of us managed to get some beer and other bottles and got just a bit loaded on the bus trip back. Getting beat 78-0 will lead to things like that. And we got busted after one of the players ended up getting stinking drunk and his parents complained to the school. Several of us admitted to our parts and got suspended for a few days, but there were others who did not step forward and were unpunished. None of us held any ill will toward them, but there was still the matter of someone taking responsibility for having obtained the liquor in the first place. Steve was the one who stepped forward and took that upon himself.

That was pretty big of him, taking the wrath of the principal of a Catholic high school. We ended up getting written up in a magazine, The Alberta Report. There was a section at the back titled "Winners and Losers." We weren't in the Winners section.

I was going to have a hockey or football career. No doubt. I went to the junior camps and played exhibition games; yet, I never thought about any of the critique given (foot speed, bad decisions under pressure ... to name a few). To me, these things were just coaches speak for their issues. It was never my fault.

I also wanted to be a rock star. It was the dawn of videos and information, and *London Calling* made me want to be Joe Strummer. I played air guitar while singing all the words to The Violent Femmes and, no, it doesn't matter that I couldn't sing or play guitar for real. In my mind, I was multi-talented.

Party-wise, I was a Weekend Warrior from 1983 through 1985. Those were good times.

When Dad got transferred again when I was in Grade 11, we ended up moving to St. Albert, near Edmonton. For some reason, that move was hard for me.

It isn't easy to move schools, but moving schools as much as we did was pretty hard. When I finally got to Grade 11, I was the big fish in that proverbial little pond and it fucking sucked to start on the bottom again.

In Grade 12, I quit playing sports all together. I ended my jocular career, cut my hair into a Mohawk, and started wearing nothing but black. I listened to alternative music and distanced myself from any fellow human beings who were not filled with angst. I would be Joe Strummer instead. This is a Radio Clash.

when i got to know steve, it became evident pretty early on that he was physically incapable of walking away from a fight.

oh, and was he deliciously angry! just that perfect percentage of bitterness flowing through his veins for me to feed on. i feed on anger. anger helps me grow. hope has the power to kill me. anger does not.

you know what else was flowing through his veins? alcohol. yes, this man had a healthy addictions problem brewing inside right around the time i met him. i love watching my victims squirm. i knew that if i didn't end up getting him, the bottle would finish the job for me.

he was struggling with his identity, i believe. he was going through a period where he liked quitting things. his guard was down.

i knew the moment as soon as I saw it.

when he stopped caring about hockey, i knew he'd stopped caring about everything. there would never be a better time.

i went straight for the jugular.

C.

5
ADRIFT

Like a boat without an anchor, without sports in my life to tether me to the ground, I started drifting. I guess I was trying to figure out where I fit in the world.

How to get along at a new school:
- *Make jokes*
- *Pick a fight with someone you can take*
- *Be extra vicious to make a point*
- *Apologize sometime later*

I refer to my senior year in high school as my Judd Nelson phase. Goodbye jock, hello rock. I was the new person at a new school, so adopting this new persona, complete with a defeatist attitude, was obviously the way to go about winning friends.

I would try something new, and then I would quit it.

I would sign up for hockey camp, and then just leave.

I'd start to play basketball, then say fuck it and not show up for practices.

I also didn't give a shit about school.

Quit this. Quit that.

I remember being in my truck in the parking lot of my high school, sleeping off the night before when my social studies teacher knocked on the window reminding me that I was late to write the provincial exam.

I had a 49% going into this test and I ended up getting an 89% on the exam to put me in a passing position. That just proves I was a sharp kid; I was just too stupid to apply myself.

I managed to pass, but I didn't have enough credits to get into university or college. I just didn't care enough to study.

I did not care about anything and I don't know what was wrong with me. I suspect it was probably some form of rebellion against all of the moving—a way to lash out at my parents. But in retrospect, I probably should just have had my fucking arse kicked.

There was one thing that I cared about. A girl I'd met while waiting for Kevin in the hallway one day. I was attracted to Anne for her beauty and her heart. She was attracted to the rebel without a cause. I asked her to a school dance and that's where it started.

From Barb

Steve was in Junior High when we were living in Dartmouth. During a parent–teacher interview the principal said to me, "You know, Steven has more general knowledge than any other student who has ever gone through this school."

We travelled a lot and I think that did him some good. He reads a lot. He's always reading. Every Sunday after church, Don and I would take the boys somewhere to buy books for them. Steve has always been a good reader. I think that's how he got through it all.

6
ATLANTIC CANADA

In 1987, I found out my parents were moving to Sydney, Cape Breton. I thought I might as well go with them and get the extra credits I needed to go back to school.

There was nothing really keeping me in Alberta. I couldn't get into university. I had some offers to play hockey, but there was nothing concrete.

I was dating Anne, but that wasn't enough to keep me there.

When we were settled in Cape Breton, I noticed a little lump on my neck. It was about the size of a piece of bubble gum.

I was having a small surgery done on my knee around that time and I ended up getting the lump removed at the same time. The doctors said the lump was benign. Nothing to worry about. That was good.

The whole thing was fairly insignificant in our lives at the time. I remember, though, the stitches came out too soon for my knee and the wound opened right up again while I was walking up the stairs one day.

There have been a lot of fucking scars since then, let
me tell you.

But anyway, it was no big deal. We were all told that
the lump was nothing to worry about, so we didn't worry
about it. I continued to drink too much and sleep until
the afternoon most days.

Now that I have some perspective, I believe I'd probably gotten a bit of a scare. Or at least enough to make
me depressed.

So much for going back to school for credits,that would
have gotten in the way of my drinking and sleeping all
day, a pattern of behaviour that was most likely killing
my parents. Though I really didn't care much about that
at the time.

steve had so much going for him. there was so much that attracted me to him. so much that made me dig in my heels. to take my stance and give him the battle of a lifetime.

it's always a gamble, taking someone with a strong support system. sometimes all that positive energy helps the victim to hold firm. to fight. but when that fails to work and i win, i love the misery of the people left behind. i don't need to destroy your cells to destroy you. i can simply take someone you love. then i have ruined you, too.

i love it when they think they have nothing to worry about. in steve's case, i initially appeared as benign. i do that sometimes.

put up a false front. hide and then jump out and surprise everyone.

not like a happy surprise. nobody likes to see me jump out from behind the curtain.

steve was a kid with no coping skills. and he absolutely hated himself. a winning combination if i'd ever seen one.

i recall thinking it might be too easy to ruin his life. that maybe it wasn't the challenge i was looking for. but then i would remember why i first chose him. i was looking for a fight. And so was he.

C.

7
ALBERTA

AFTER MY SURGERY, I decided to move back out west. I had a tendency to move a lot, back then. Maybe I was conditioned to do so with all of the moves we made when I was growing up. I believe I just thought I could lose my problems if I changed my surroundings.

To anyone reading this today, that decision to move out west might not seem like a very big deal. There are pretty mass migrations of people from eastern Canada to the west these days. But back then, that was kind of a major thing to do—to move 5,000 miles away from home.

I was only eighteen years old and I was on my own. Anne was sticking around, by some miracle. During the years that would follow my high school graduation when I didn't know where I fit, Anne became a social connection. She was a haven that I would run to, to help ride through the storms.

Eventually, that beautiful blond girl with the sparkling eyes would become the hostage of her alcoholic husband.

We continued dating and I moved in with my cousin. He wasn't very fun. At least he didn't see the humor in having me around. He was a police officer with the city of

Edmonton and he instated a pretty strict curfew, which I had a problem conforming to.

I was living it up. Partying pretty hard. Not following the rules of the house. I remember getting home late one night and puking all over the place. That was not cool of me. The guy had small children and nobody needs to see that.

It wasn't long before I'd worn out my welcome and had to find myself another place to live. I ended up moving in to a friend's house. I think my parents ended up giving them money to basically take care of me for them.

I was drunk all the time.

Anne was going to university and getting great grades. I couch surfed. I audited some classes at U of A. But I was basically a royal mess. Dad had retired from the RCMP and was working as Chief of the Charlottetown City Police in PEI. I moved to Halifax to be a bit closer to them and to get away from myself for awhile.

And then that lump came back.

Except this time, it was the size of a golf ball. I went to visit Mom and Dad and they could see the lump in my neck from a hundred paces away.

I got the lump all checked out by a doctor there in Charlottetown. We told the doctor about that first lump I'd had removed in Sydney. The doctor called about getting a copy of that file from the surgeon who performed the surgery. I didn't think anything else of it.

Not until a couple days later when I got a phone call. I was sitting down drinking a beer with a friend when the phone rang.

A note in my file said that the original lumpectomy should have been followed up on, but that fell through the cracks.

Steve, you have Hodgkins Disease. That's a type of cancer.

Well that's shitty, I remember thinking.

Hodgkins has an 85% cure rate. You'll need radiation for a few months and you'll be done.

I was nineteen, so I didn't think I could die. I sort of panicked, but then I went out, got a pack of smokes and a six-pack of beer, and continued with my evening.

Mom and Dad were concerned, but we weren't too worried. None of us had really heard about Hodgkins before. Had no idea what it was.

There was that 15% statistic though—those who don't survive Hodgkins—, so I was forced to face my own mortality, and Mom and Dad were probably forced to think about what would happen if their son died before they did, but it wasn't something we dwelled on. Anne took it in stride, too, and she stuck around to continue on with our long-distance love affair. It was life as usual. There was no other option besides me going for treatment and fighting the disease.

This was 1989. Treatment meant radiation therapy in Halifax. Radiation kills cancer cells, but it also obliterates healthy tissue. The theory is, since normal tissue is healthier than cancer cells, it will be able to fix itself when treatment is through.

Radiation itself doesn't hurt. It makes you pretty nauseous when it's over, but being shot with laser beams isn't painful.

I remember, though, I did happen to have the worst technician on the planet administer the dye for my radiation treatment. That hurt. And I still have the scars.

In order for the doctors to see where things are, they need to have a technician inject you with this blue dye. They do this by pumping dye through your feet. First they freeze your feet, and then they cut a slit in there to stick in a needle to inject the dye.

There wasn't enough freezing for my dye job and I will never forget the feeling of that razor cutting through my feet.

The first sign of the stigmata, without the benefits of being a prophet.

Later that night, I went out drinking in Halifax.

Hey, I bet you $10 if I drink this Labatt's Blue, I'll pee blue.

I was living with a friend who was going to Saint Mary's. I had started auditing some classes, but I continued to party pretty hard. Especially for a dude getting radiation therapy.

I actually wasn't taking the whole radiation/cancer thing very seriously, and it caught up to me eventually. I started getting tired and sick, and I was forced to slow down about four months after treatment started.

When my treatment was over, I moved back to Charlottetown with Mom and Dad.

I cut down a bit on the drinking and the smoking. I started eating home cooking and playing hockey again.

By that time, at the age of twenty, I'd say I was an alcoholic.

I would also say that from age twenty to twenty-seven, I was adrift, lost, and lonesome.

Part of it was the alcohol; part of it was the cancer. Part of it was most definitely Post-Traumatic Stress Disorder, and part of it was depression.

Most of it was me trying to escape from myself.

During the 1990s, my brother and one of our best buddies, Ward, were commissioned on several occasions to go to a place where I'd been living and pack up all my shit to put it in storage.

Many times they had to go into places where I had gotten myself kicked out, which was probably really pleasant for them. Cleaning up another one of my messes.

But they were my friends and they put up with me. They didn't like it, but they put up with it. They know I would have done the same for them.

Nothing Star

Write it down for yourself
It's a nothing star
Let the rain come inside
The bird on the lawn
Is right where it's supposed to be

And all this goes on
And I'm not a celebrity

Everything is exactly where
It's supposed to be
And I'm not a celebrity

The harbor is still
Music taking me where I want to go
Let the wind stir up the trees
Cigarettes heighten the emotion
The cars pass bye

And all this goes on
And I'm not a celebrity

No I'm not
Or will ever be
A celebrity

From Kevin

I really liked it when Steve was around. He moved around so much that it was nice when he would settle long enough in the city in which I was living so we could hang out. But gradually I started to notice that he was drinking a lot more than the rest of us. And it wasn't having a good effect on him.

He was pretty mouthy when he was drinking and he had a real talent for finding trouble when he was drunk. I don't think he ever actually looked for it, but it sure found him.

It got to the point where I didn't like being around him when he was drinking. I was always worrying about him and I was worried about his mouth getting us into a situation that we couldn't handle.

In the early 1990s, Steve and I were having a beer at Don Cherry's in Edmonton with a mutual friend.

Steve was hammered. He was pounding the beer back and he kept on ordering pitchers. I was drinking an insane amount of the draft beer to prevent him from drinking more because I knew he was going to try to drive home.

The bartender ended up cutting us off. Before we left, I caught sight of Steve at the bar trying to convince him to give him a Rum & Coke to go.

That night, it was pretty clear that things had spiraled out of control.

8
ADDICTION

I HAVE REALLY LIKED alcohol ever since I was that awkward thirteen year old. Alcohol, however, does not like me.

When I was a teenager, I drank a lot. I didn't drink to feel good, though. I drank to hurt myself. I drank hard and I drank often. I would drink until I couldn't drink anymore. Then I would throw up and start again.

When does one cross the line from being someone who likes to get drunk to being someone who needs to get drunk? I don't know when that was for me (I'd guess late teens), but I do know that I didn't drink to be social. Getting drunk was always the goal. Anne didn't think much of it, but I didn't really care.

Alcoholics become addicted at the mental level because it does something for us. We begin to think that the effects of alcohol are reasonable ways to escape our true feelings. It all boils down to that. If we're sad, we drink to get a buzz and forget the sadness. If we're angry, we drink to get back at whoever angered us. If we're happy, we drink to elevate the happiness. If we're shy, we drink to become more confident. If we have low self-esteem, we drink to raise our sense of self-worth.

This mental exercise becomes so ingrained in us and the habit has then been firmly established.

Eventually, we drink only to keep the buzz, so we can't have just one drink. We must drink to get drunk. We must eventually drink to live.

I know this now, but I didn't then. I actually ended up in the emergency room at one point. I was having short-ness of breath and chest pains. I was twenty years old, so it was clear I wasn't having a heart attack. I was made to breathe into a paper bag because what I was actually having was an alcohol-induced panic attack.

Good times.

I moved back out west then and continued drifting from couch to couch, from disgusting apartment to nice apartment. Hockey tryouts, Anne, drinking, reading books, watching movies. Back to PEI, back to Alberta. Drinking, movies, sleeping. There was no structure, except that I was a vagabond and I could be counted on to get into fights and to lie while I was drinking.

I was a mean drunk. And I knew that I was an asshole when I was drinking, but it did not stop me.

This reckless, stupid behaviour went on for three years. I was getting to the point of realizing that it wasn't the healthiest lifestyle to maintain.

So, what did I decide to do?

Get married of course, to Anne, because when you get married, the bullshit comes to an end. You get a house with a white picket fence and you settle down.

Man. I was so fucking smart at twenty-three.

My new bride's father was wealthy. He set us up in St. Albert in a nice little apartment. I got myself a sales job and I was pretty good at it. I was better at the drinking after work part of the job, though, which took place at the Don Cherry's Bar across the parking lot.

I was drunk all the time. I kept telling Anne that I would quit. She somehow put up with the lying and the cheating and the stealing long enough to get pregnant. We didn't think that would be possible with all the radiation I'd had.

Surprise! Happy, happy surprise.

Despite the drinking, I was doing well at my job. Well enough, in fact, that I was asked to be manager of a big box electronics store in Kelowna, BC. I happily accepted the new position (I did love to move, after all!).

We were expecting a baby, I had gotten a promotion, and we were living in a nice condo village full of young couples and old people—newly wed and nearly dead.

God, grant me the serenity to accept the things I cannot change, the courage to change the things I can, and the wisdom to know the difference.

As a practicing alcoholic for many years, I had no desire to try to better myself in any way, physically, mentally, or spiritually. It was all about getting my next drink—my life revolved around booze, and anything else, be it work, friendships, or my health, was an inconvenience.

I also frowned upon anyone else who might be trying to better themselves.

People who went to the gym—they were wasting their time. I could be a star hockey player if I wanted to be.

People who studied hard—I was smarter than they were and I didn't need a diploma to tell me that.

People who said they lived a spiritual life, people who were sober, people in general—the list went on ad nauseam. I know now that I was jealous of those who had their lives together, and I dealt with that by putting them down. Even while I was looking up from the gutter, my alcoholic mind still told me I was better than the people standing on the sidewalk.

Anne continued to ask me to quit drinking, and as an alcoholic and a liar, I promised her that I would.

She left to go visit friends in Vancouver, BC, one weekend and I decided to get drunk and follow her. She was visiting my buddy Ward and his wife. They were my friends, too, after all.

Besides, I was never very good by myself.

I told everyone at work that my wife was ill and I needed to get to Vancouver to see her. It took me eleven hours to make the four-hour drive. I drank the entire way, which likely had a lot to do with it.

When I got to Vancouver and Anne saw me there at Ward's doorstep, her face contorted into this look that can only be described as disappointment. I was obviously in no shape to have been driving. She needed a break from me and there I was. She had probably spent her visit up until that point talking about what bad shape I was in. I helped her prove her point.

I convinced Ward to go out drinking at Dick's on Dicks with me. (Richard's on Richards—best name for a bar, ever.) When we were leaving the bar, I stole a 40-ouncer before we headed back to Ward's place.

My wife was seven months pregnant, and Ward and his wife had a new baby at home.

I was caught by Ward's wife, hiding in the closet at 10:00 the next morning making love to that 40-ouncer, pouring it down my throat, trying to maintain the buzz from the night before.

You could say that was a low point.

It didn't really get much better for a little while after that. I thought I was doing a pretty good job hiding all the drinking from my boss, but of course he knew what was going on.

I would come back from lunch smelling like booze. I would come into work looking pretty rough after a hard night out. The regional manager was less than impressed with all the drinking. He threatened to fire me, so I quit. Not the job, the drinking.

I was twenty-five years old at that point and I stopped drinking. And then I became a dry drunk. A workaholic.

Everyone was happy.

My wife started going to Al-Anon to try to get some support. She started getting after me to go to AA. I wanted nothing to do with it.

I'm not fucking drinking, so leave me alone.

She got empowered by the support group and she wouldn't leave me alone about going to AA meetings.

I told her I was going to keep her quiet, and I would usually just drive around for an hour.

Then my daughter Kelsey was born.

October 5, 1993. A golden day.

Mom and Dad came out to Kelowna to be there for the birth. I made $9,000 in commissions over the holidays and was named salesman of the year. I was in my element. By the time spring rolled around a few months later, I still hadn't started drinking again.

In the spring of 1994, I went to see the doctor because I was feeling pretty shitty. I thought I had pneumonia.

The doctor took an x-ray. It showed that my body was full of tumors.

The cancer was back and I was not equipped to handle it.

Hyde

That black irish humour
Held the day
But not the night

Forever, Forboding, Unforgiving
Tap the floor
Bottle the rage

There he is
Shaking the cage
Shaking that goddam cage

Insistent, Insidious, Insane
Tap the keg
Bottle the rage

There he is
Out of his cage
Out of his fucking cage

He's not going back in
He's not at that stage

So stand back
Be well aware
He's out of his cage
He's out of his cage

it's fun when they think they've got me beat and i continue to hide.

olly olly oxen free!

it rarely happens that people beat me twice. a lot of
people are smart enough to just go ahead and die the
first time around. with their first encounter with me.
they're the smart ones. i am kind compared to the death
that comes from my cure.

but the weak ones are no fun. that's why i like steve so
much. why i keep on flowing through him. why i would
continue to hide and wait.

and i would wait. i have nothing but time and i can
be in more than one place at once. an evil santa claus.
but you can't return what i bring. i bring death, not easy
bake ovens.

i waited for steve to get his shit together before i
alerted him of my existence. waited for him to marry
and to bring a healthy little baby into the world.

oh! he entertained me the way he thumbed his nose
at me. the way he underestimated me.

i lay dormant in him for so long. so long. so long.

don't fucking underestimate me.

i am going to ruin you, steve, and i'm also going to
ruin that pretty little blond you're married to. no, i don't
have to inhabit someone to ruin them. by association
will do just fine.

C.

9
AGAIN

It's back.

It was never supposed to come back.

What are you talking about?

The world fell down.

Looking up from the bottom of a well.

How is this possible?

The cancer was worse than before. Fuck.

That's when my sobriety ended.

Treatment included steroids that brought out a monster. Especially while under the influence of alcohol.

* * *

The air in the bar is thick with smoke. Some of it mine.

There are two empty beer bottles beside me.

I introduce myself to number three while the girls dance for me.

Crack off the cap.

Bartender puts number four in front of me.

Condensation on the bottle.

My thoughts go for a minute to my six-month-old baby at home with her mother. My wife. Thoughts don't stay long.

I stumble home in the wee hours of the morning. Husband of the year. She's not happy to see me.

"Where have you been?" Baby drool on her shoulder. A mess of bottles and nipples line the counter.

"None of your fucking business," I smile. Go to the fridge. Look for a bottle of something stronger than Similac. Find a beer. Open it, drink it down.

"You can't just do this, Steve. You can't leave me with the baby and be out there doing God knows what! You're sick! You need to go to one of those meetings."

"Would you just shut up you goddamned bitch," I attack. "If you hadn't let yourself get so fucking huge, maybe I wouldn't have to go out and look at hot, naked girls."

I might as well have hit her with my fist.

"What's happening to you, Steve?"

"Like you could fucking begin to understand what I'm going through."

Tears come to her eyes. Her hands go to her mouth before she goes to check on the baby.

I throw up everything I drank that night. Then, I light a cigarette and crack open another beer.

I was such an asshole, so incredibly selfish. I wish I could go back and deck that guy in the apartment. Take the boots to him, smarten him up, and protect her from me. When did I disappear into the dark side?

1994 was a good year for me. i was thriving in steve. stronger than before. i had a real chance of taking him down for good this time. i was definitely ruining his marriage. my goal was to force her to leave him. they weren't really in love. it didn't look like it from where i was sitting, anyway.

but i didn't want to stop there. too risky.

who knows. maybe they did love each other enough to survive me.

just in case i needed a back up plan.

what would i do. what would i do.

then it came to me.

why didn't i think of it before? it was such a simple idea, yet it would ruin him.

i would take down someone that he loved. someone he loved as much as he loved anything or anyone in the world. someone he loved much more than he loved himself.

eeny, meeny, miny, moe...

C.

From Don

I left the RCMP after 34 years. The moving, the nature of the job—it was a long time to be in that line of work. My wife and I settled in Charlottetown where I got a job as Chief of the City Police. I retired after six years in that role.

I wasn't feeling well, but the doctor kept saying it was just stress. They couldn't find anything wrong with me.

But I knew something wasn't right. I was tired and was just feeling like crap.

Finally the doctor ordered a barium enema.

We got the result of that test on my first day of retirement. September 1, 1994.

I had colon cancer.

The oncologist said it was headed to two lymph nodes.

Treatment was to be surgery to remove the cancer, followed by 53 weeks of chemotherapy.

I couldn't help but wonder why this was happening to my family.

I moved in with Kevin in Edmonton to start treatment for the cancer. I was on a chemotherapy and prednisone regimen. I know now that I had at least a touch of PTSD. I was fucked up mentally and physically.

At that same time, Dad was fighting his own battle back in PEI. Even though I was probably too sick to travel, I flew home to be there for his bowel surgery in September.

That meant a lot to him.

In December, he asked his doctors if he could take a break from his 53-week chemo regime so that he could visit with Kevin and me for the holidays.

The clinic arranged for Dad to get his weekly treatment while he was visiting me. The image of me and Dad sitting there side-by-side on recliners getting our chemo together was Cancer's version of a Hallmark card. Not exactly watching a football game together.

I think we drew on each other's strength.

When treatment was over, it was back to BC. Even though I was sober throughout my treatment, Anne kept bringing up what I had said and done when I was drinking. Over and over.

I guess I loved her. I believed I did at the time. We'd been together for nine years; yet, we were never really close. I don't think we ever really knew each other.

Sometimes I would look at her and I would wish I could be someone else so that we could be happy, but I don't know if that would have worked or not. I'll never know.

I liked being married to Anne, but the addict inside hated the hours and the "being at home" requirements. I told too many lies and said too many nasty things for there to be any hope of us staying together.

We separated and she left. I don't blame her for leaving. It took courage for her to do that and I applaud her decision. I wear that guilt to this day. What I regret most was that I missed so much time with my daughter. I don't get to have that back.

I sometimes wonder if Anne wears any guilt of her own. For choosing the "in sickness" time in my life to leave. Could I have been saved if she stayed? Would her love and support have ever been enough to take me off that brink? To talk me down off the ledge?

The night Anne left, I sat on the patio with a bottle of vodka, a bottle of wine, and a dozen beer. I drank myself into a stupor.

Blue Rodeo was playing on the stereo and I was trying to figure out how I would get her back.

I know. I'll send her flowers. She loves flowers. They always work.

It was too late, though.

Everyone knows that glass, once shattered, can never be put back together again.

From Barb

I never let myself think that he wouldn't be okay. I knew he would get better and I said the same thing about Don when he was sick. It was a terrible time, but I never let myself think, "this is it." That wouldn't have done any good. They were going to be okay. That's all I kept thinking in my head and in my heart. It didn't hurt that I had prayers coming for both of them from here to Texas.

PART TWO
1995–2009

It Feels Ominous

The night ahead
I know what's bothering me
I just don't want to say it out loud
The feeling is constant
It won't go away
I know what's been eating at me
I just don't want to say it out loud
For richer or poorer
In sickness and in health
Time for to get leaving
Time to look out for myself
The acceptance comes later
It settles down inside
We all know where it's going
We just don't want to say it out loud
For richer or poorer
In sickness and in health
Time for you to get leaving

Time for me to look out for self

Car Seat

The snow came gently down
All around
My old stomping grounds

I carried my child into the night
Streetlight,
Something didn't feel right

It was supposed to be
You and me,
And baby makes three

The boots by the door weren't mine,
Just fine,
Now I walk a straight line.

I send the child back into my old life
Old wife
Internal strife.

It was supposed to be
You and me,
And baby makes three

It was supposed to be
You and me,
And baby makes three

From Don

Steve is a terrible patient. But with all the drugs and everything else that he was going through, well, you can only put up with so much. He must have been saying to himself, "Why me? Why me again?" But never has he spoken that out loud. He is the strongest person I have ever met in my life.

Rogers Pass

My eyes are open
But I'm asleep
Sun's behind the mountain now
She looked across
Couldn't get the passage out

Somewhere in that valley
It was never in doubt

My state was more profound
Then sleep
Darkness beckons stars
He looked across
Couldn't get the passage out

Somewhere in the valley
It was never in doubt

The night doubles as silence
There is nothing left to say
The dawn traces the line cross
We looked at each other
Couldn't get a passage out

Somewhere in the valley
Probably at the start of the road
It was never in doubt

10
ALONE

WITH THE CANCER back and my marriage over, I ended up drifting again. Mom and Dad were in PEI. Dad's cancer was gone, thank God. Kevin was in Edmonton. Good reliable Kevin. He never did leave Alberta. I have trouble relating to that contentment to stay in one place.

Anne took our little girl and moved from Kelowna to live with her parents in Edmonton.

I was in BC by myself, working and getting chemo treatments.

Work mattered. Getting better mattered.

I had lost everything else.

The best sobering-up plan I found was cancer treatment. Drinking while going through chemo is a pretty fucking bad idea.

I was so sick that I just couldn't drink.

When they say the cure is worse than the disease, they aren't making that shit up.

If you don't know what chemo involves, basically it's the use of intravenous drugs and/or chemical agents to kill cancerous cells. There are different types of drugs and different regimes for different times of cancers.

The thing about cancer cells is that the scientists still haven't figured out how to target them, so the poison they put in you kills all your cells in an effort to get the bad ones. That's why you lose your hair and your body fat. Usually you get one cycle a month for eight months. With each session, you sit under a blanket for a couple of hours, hooked up to an IV with all kinds of drugs going into you. Or if you're lucky, you might also get some platelets or a blood transfusion at the same time. You're given some anti-nausea drugs to go home with.

In between sessions, you're tested to see if any progress is being made. Part of the regimen for me was prednisone steroids and a type of mustard gas.

After my eighth and final treatment in BC, I moved back to Edmonton. That was January of 1995. I was cured. And, since the treatment was over, I could drink again! I celebrated with beer and pizza and I proceeded to throw up all night. The end of a cycle is hard.

At this time, my buddy Ward was battling demons of his own. He was actually in a 12-step group for gambling addicts and he kept encouraging me to get help for my drinking.

Of course, I didn't think I needed help.

I was happy to keep getting drunk and when I was sober, I would go to see my daughter and try to prove to my ex-wife that I'd changed. I was lonely and I missed Anne and the baby.

One night, I went out and got piss drunk and ended up back at her house. She asked if I could take care of my daughter for a little while and I said I couldn't. I was drunk.

At that point, we both knew it was the end of our relationship.

I moved back to BC because that's what I did when things weren't going well for me. My old boss took me back and I found a roommate.

It was my own fault that I was alone.

I'd fucked everything up all by myself. I was pissing off everyone I loved.

I was driving them all away.

But it still hurt.

I couldn't hold on to a job. I couldn't keep a woman around. I was detached from everything and everyone.

I wished that I had someone to talk to. Someone who could help me work through the shit I was going through. I didn't care about anything except my daughter. I had no interest in hockey anymore. I couldn't sleep. I had no appetite. I was irritable and angry at everything and everyone. I guess I wasn't interested in life. All of these things, we know now were symptoms of PSTD. I had no coping mechanisms.

But I guess we didn't know as much then as we do now.

   i thought the irony of trying to take his father was beautiful. didn't work though. tough fucking man that was. if he hadn't had that surgeon. if they'd been only a couple weeks later finding me, i would have been throughout his lymphatic system and he'd have been mine.

   the plan may even have backfired. steve seems stronger than ever before.

   i need another plan.

11
ANGST

THAT JUDD NELSON phase I went through in high school was just a bit of foreshadowing of what was to come.

I was filled with angst for many years of my youth.

I loved the music of the early 1990s. Nirvana, Hole. The more pain in the music, the better. I loved being miserable.

Since I drank to hurt myself, I thought it would be a good idea to celebrate my twenty-seventh birthday by getting drunk.

I drank all the beer in the fridge, and I drank it until I threw up and then I switched to the hard stuff. Then, to the bar. Tequila for everyone! I continued drinking into the night. I came home with someone I didn't know, but after I managed to take the rubber plant in the foyer and beat the living piss out of it, she decided to leave. Can't imagine why.

I woke to regret, guilt, and absolute helplessness. There was a hole inside me that had been there for a while. I couldn't get the taste of the night before out of my mouth.

I decided I was done.

I packed up my stuff again, which at this point was basically some CDs, ball caps, and a few t-shirts.

I was feeling pretty sorry for myself.

I was still half drunk when I started out on the Coqui-halla Highway, one of the most dangerous roads in Canada, in the dead of winter in a little Jeep that was no doubt not winter-ready in any way. When I finally got to Edmonton, I realized I needed a place to stay. Kevin wasn't in town, so I called Ward.

I could hear the negotiation going on in the background with his wife. She knew that I was fucked up. She hadn't forgotten about finding me in the closet making out with a 40-ouncer of rum.

She finally agreed, after much groveling on Ward's part, to let me stay with them. My ex brought our little girl over so I could see her. Nobody was very happy with me. I was a fuck up, and we all knew it.

On March 12, 1995, Kevin and Ward took me out for breakfast. I remember the date because it was my intervention.

Over bacon and eggs, they told me that if I didn't get my shit together, as much as they loved me, they wanted nothing more to do with me.

So, they bought me a pack of smokes and a copy of *The Razor's Edge* by Maugham (my favourite book), and drove me to detox.

Known Forecast

The wind whistles a tune
I've heard before.
The sun shone on a spot I knew.
I was happy and so were you.
Yeah, I was happy,
And so were you.

The darkness covered the storm inside.
The clouds rolled through narrow halls.

The sky smiled as I remembered.
The sun shone on a spot I knew.
I was happy,
And so were you.
Yeah,
For a moment I was happy,
And so were you.

The thunder rolled in from the east.
The rain poured throughout the house.
I wasn't happy and neither were you.
Neither were you.

12

ALCOHOLICS ANONYMOUS

WHEN'S THE LAST time you drank?

"Uh . . . 48 hours."

We're sorry, we can't take you.

"Excuse me?"

You have to have been drinking within the last 24 hours in order for us to take you.

"My friends are trying to help me, and you want me to go get polluted and come back?"

Gotta love that system.

They told me to go to an Alcoholics Anonymous meeting in St. Albert and I actually went this time.

I crushed my cigarette under my foot, pulled the brim of my Notre Dame cap to the tip of my nose, and walked into a room full of alcoholics.

There was someone there who I knew from high school. He was talking about all of these great things that were going on in his life.

I stayed quiet myself, but that meeting gave me hope, so I kept going back. If that guy from high school could do it, maybe I could, too.

It was the last house on the block and the only one that would let me in with all my baggage.

The people inside that room saved my life. They offered hope, a different way of living, and the power of example.

I kept coming back to the meetings. I got a sponsor, a boy name Shannon, whose biological family came from Souris, PEI—the same place my biological family came from. All roads lead back to Souris.

I followed orders, cleaned the ashtrays, and followed the twelve steps.

The meetings themselves helped heal me in some way that I don't think anyone but another addict knows. It's mixed up magic.

The meetings afterward were even more magical. Gathering at the local coffee shop, we would talk and talk about feelings and problems and all the stuff I hadn't talked about in a long time to anyone. I didn't have to be someone I wasn't.

That was 1995. I've been sober ever since.

One long day, one short day at a time.

13
ABYSS

I GOT A CRAPPY apartment in Edmonton.

Ward had a hand in saving my life. I wish I could have saved his.

Ward was having his own struggles. He and his wife had split up and he was missing his daughter as much as I was missing mine.

He got kicked out of his apartment because he couldn't pay the rent, and he moved in with me about a month after I'd settled into my new place. He knew the deal was that he had to have his share of the rent by the end of the month or he couldn't stay there.

He and Kevin and I had a couple other buddies who we got around with. We were a tight pack of friends.

We loved going out and watching improv comedy shows, listening to live music, and watching football and hockey games.

We all knew that Ward liked gambling. He was always borrowing money from us, but he always paid it back. His problem wasn't directly affecting us, so we didn't really need to interfere. But then, the amounts started getting bigger and the period of time between loans got shorter.

Suddenly, he was having trouble coming up with rent money.

One night, I caught him playing poker in St. Albert, and I told him he needed to get his act together.

It was apparent that things were getting out of hand when he started selling off his power tools to make money because he built kitchens for a living.

Kevin and I ended up having a bit of a Come To Jesus with Ward in the winter of 1997, two years after my own intervention. We wanted to know what he was spending all the money on, but he was an expert liar. He knew how to manipulate us and how to shut us up.

He called Kevin one Tuesday asking him if he wanted to go for coffee. Kevin had to work, so he told Ward to call him back on Friday.

Ward never called Kevin back, but his brother called Kevin asking him if he'd seen Ward. Ward had taken his mother's car and had taken off.

I got a call on Easter Saturday from Kevin. He'd heard back from Ward's brother. He didn't have to tell me what had happened.

Ward's eyes were always so sad.

I knew he had finally gone. He'd killed himself.

He needed relief from his mind, the unbearable lightness of being.

I see from above, a car in a wheat field. I feel the silence. It's so fucking quiet. Someone scream out! A tragedy has taken place.

The thought of him all alone in that field haunts me to this day. I think it always will. I loved him and we had gone through so much together.

A friend told me once that the weirdest thing about when someone dies is walking outside after the funeral. The world continues and moves at the same pace.

I still talk to him sometimes. I always think of him when I hear his favourite song. I should listen to that song more often. "Listen to the mandolin rain, listen to my heartbreak..." (Bruce Hornsby).

Ward

When you sleep my friend
Sleep in stars
Walk up Orion
Slide down the Big Dipper
But whether near or far, sleep in stars

14
AUTOLOGOUS BONE
MARROW TRANSPLANT

SOMETHING'S NOT RIGHT.

I entertain my fear by going over the checklist:

Temp: 98.8. Acceptable

Pulse: 90. A little high, but sick is 150. I'll take it

Fingertips: Pink. Not anemic

Lower shins: Clear of red freckles that indicate low platelets

I lie on my back.

Breathe in.

Breathe out.

Hands pushed under my left ribcage feeling for something I hope I won't find.

Spleen: Normal

Nice.

I feel sort of certain that my symptoms are less likely to be as a result of lymphoma.

Symptoms of Post-Traumatic Stress Disorder

- Loss of interest in activities and life in general
- Irritability interrupted by outbursts of anger
- Intense physical reactions to reminders of the event
- Inability to remember important aspects of the trauma
- Avoiding reminders of the trauma
- Re-experiencing the event
- Feeling detached from others
- Feeling emotionally numb
- Feeling frightened, sad, anxious
- Depression and hopelessness
- Sense of a limited future
- Constant sense of danger
- Difficulty concentrating
- Difficulty sleeping
- Painful memories
- Increased anxiety
- Flashbacks
- Nightmares
- Feeling jumpy
- Feeling alienated

In 1997, I moved back to Atlantic Canada. I was in Charlottetown, PEI, where my parents were at the time. I was being led around like a puppy by my PTSD. I was in a deep depression after Ward committed suicide.

I went to the mental health clinic because I really needed to talk to someone. I sat across from the counsellor and started spilling my guts: *Moved around all my life ... Found a lump when twenty years ago that was supposedly benign ... Ended up being Hodgkins Disease ... Chemo, radiation ... Married, baby ... Cancer came back ... Addiction problems ... Divorced ... Sobered up ... Best friend committed suicide.*

Brain dominates blood, I would whisper to myself.

The counsellor questioned how one person could survive all of that and made a comment about how I was doing good just to get myself there to the clinic.

That wasn't a lot of help. I was waiting for a prize for being the most fucked up person to come through the door that year.

Brain dominates blood, I would whisper to myself.

My family was trying to help get me out of the funk I was in. I ended up getting a job in Halifax in the brand new world of the Internet—it fit me like a glove. Fine by me! I was due for another move. I started going to AA meetings there, and I met a guy with a bad attitude and general disdain for rules. I liked him immediately and to this day, he's my best friend.

I was doing well at my job. I ended up getting a promotion, which involved all kinds of benefits including a couple of computers and a car allowance. Things were looking up.

In early 1998, I did have a health scare with a lesion on my chest. It was tested and, according to the doctors, it was benign.

Good.

In August, I had a follow up. Wasn't too concerned about it.

When the blood work came back, I got a call while I was on the road for work, driving around some big wig mucky muck from Toronto. We were on our way to Truro.

Steve, your potassium level is through the roof.

Fuck. (I think this is bad)

Come to the hospital immediately.

No.

You are in danger of dying.

I needed a bone marrow transplant. The cancer was back.

Acceptance is key. Acceptance is key. That's what they say in AA.

From Bobby (Best friend)

Steve and I met through AA in 1998 when he'd moved back to Nova Scotia from Alberta. I was his sponsor. At one meeting, I was on a rant about something or other. I had a short fuse for bullshit. Steve came up to me after the meeting and told me that I'd said all the things he was thinking of saying but was afraid to because he was new.

I remember being taken aback by his directness.

We had the same dry sense of humor. We liked hockey and we were competitive.

We hit it off right away.

He kept most of his personal history to himself, not that he hid it or was ashamed of it, but he didn't share much about his health struggles. As his sponsor, I distinctly remember asking him if he'd be okay. If he'd be okay dealing with the illness sober. He said that if he thought a drink was going to make this better, he'd have had one already.

I've worked with a lot of different people as an addictions counsellor and a lot of people who've been adopted have had issues. There's often an underlying issue that goes back to a dysfunctional sense of love and loyalty and a family of origin thing. That couldn't be further from the truth in Steve's case. He always said there was no demon in his closet on the adoption front.

But Steve has had a demon of another sort that keeps rearing its ugly head, stopping him in his tracks. He has no control over that and I think that's one of his fears. That his health is out of his control.

It has happened so many times. Life seems to be going great then the Earth shakes from underneath him and he has to suck it up and do the do again.

after steven and i had been together for ten years, i wanted to do something special to commemorate the occasion.

besides. i had grown tired of waiting for him to dive back into the bottle. i tried to break him down. tried to make him give up hope on humanity, but he just wouldn't give up. fucking faith.

i swear that daughter of his is partly to blame for him fighting so hard. if she wasn't in the picture, things would be different.

so ten years after his "benign" tumor had been removed, i came back to visit.

here i am! i've got you this time.

i want to play.

C.

Time for the doctor's appointment. Is my blood count up? How much cancer has left my body? Can they do the transplant? When can we do the transplant? Is there a match?

When your chance for a cure goes from 50% to 10%, with or without a procedure, you tend to get worked up about the outcome and guess, worry, and pray.

I guessed and I worried. I prayed and I promised. I promised and prayed.

Bone marrow rescue.

Since there was no match for a donor, they did an autologous bone marrow transplant—a procedure to harvest my own stem cells to inject them back into me. Painful as hell. They took my bone marrow out and shipped it to California where it was cleaned. Then, it was shipped back and put back into me.

***

Find the energy from somewhere to open my eyelids. Grip the sides of the mattress. Grimace. Struggle to get up out of bed.

Tubes hang from my chest and I reach for needles. Pull at the needles.

After the bone marrow transplant, it felt like I'd clawed outside of my own carcass and jumped up and down on that bag of bones until I just couldn't take it anymore. The pain was bad enough to make you vomit and black out.

After a bone marrow transplant, you're like a wounded animal looking for a cave to crawl into just to be left alone.

Insert fluid.

Clean.

Breakfast of champions.

Need cigarette, must have cigarette. Wonder if I could smoke through the tube?

I didn't expect, at age thirty, to be a three-time cancer victim.

Divorced.

A recovering drunk whose best friend had killed himself.

I call the young one. She is like me, only beautiful.

The eyes are mine, not hers, not her mother's. They reflect me. Her father. The man who runs. The man who left her to another one to mind her, to teach her.

"Cleanse me, my darling. Give a piece of heaven to this fallen angel."

"Dad, don't!" she says, as I tease her.

Heal my ills lord so I can see her again.

There are no atheists in foxholes.

"I have to go Dad, call me on Tuesday," the words drifted off into mist.

"Love you, Darling, I love you," my voice is a whisper and the world stops for a brief second. My house is 3000 miles from my home.

Days drag days with them when one battles illness. The battle back to normalcy seems eternal. There is nobody to share the intimate thoughts with. Parents try to be spouses, but even though you value the attempted substitution, the boundaries still remain intact. Gratitude comes begrudgingly.

> *The value of hope*
> *The distance of view*
> *The season of no meaning*
> *The spirit seeks refuge*

When you aren't working, you forget how it fills you. Not only in remuneration, but also with dignity and ambition and a sense of placement in the world. Saying that, there is only so much time suckage one can manufacture, especially when the world is in a constant spin.

The room you're in is 10×10 and sterile and plastic. The squeak of sensible rubber soled shoes on linoleum tile. Of carts rolling by. Beeps. Paging Dr. So-And-So.

The walls get closer together everyday. The gray fades to gray.

They give you morphine. Oh, beautiful morphine! Your room turns into a different scene constantly.

> *Pizza parlor in Brooklyn.*
> *The Ice at Northlands Coliseum.*
> *A brothel in Rome (my personal favourite).*

I need more morphine.

> *The waves crash into me.*
> *I see the waves crash into me.*

They came one-by-one to the mountain. The boy lies clinging to his toy.

"Take me away from this place! Please take me away from this place..." He cries and seeks his father.

Olympic vomit throws. I qualified. Judge from the nursing station gives me a 9.5.

Oh, how I hate myself for leaving. Or in truth, making her leave with the young one.

My nurse just won the drag queen contest at the local gay bar. He was a very attractive woman.

Too bad the utensils were different.

He tells me the sicker you are, the better the recovery you have. If that's the case, I'll be doing Got milk? ads once I leave this godforsaken place.

When there was nobody else in the room and it was just me, a bag of bones, anxiety would strike and I entered the world of Can't Sit Down. Can't Stand Up. Drugs. Drugs. Drugs. Population: One.

Horse tranquilizers required.

The night awaits the damned.

When locked in a small room and fed a steady diet of narcotics, your emotions can go from despair to bountiful hope all in the period of an hour. You hang on the doctors' and nurses' every word. Analyze and draw conclusions.

Your world bounces back and forth.
Back and forth.
Back and forth.

The world seems so far away when you have a tube stuck in your neck and blood flowing in and out of you like some type of grotesque water fountain.

You have to pee and your dignity is handed to you in the form of a bedpan.

The thoughts of your life flash back and forth.

Sticking needles in your stomach to increase the blood cell count.

"Amazing. Glory, Glory Hallelujah!"

The things you think about are the things you love.

"Where is my baby girl?"

The hallucinations were horrific.

I wasn't in isolation.

I was in Hell.

The ones you love
The fullness of home
The laughter of your child
The places you've roamed
The lining of your coffin.

The soundtrack in your head
The light feels warm skin is all shed

It's so funny how
You're not so funny now
It's so ironic
You've created your own tonic

How you ran away from what you wanted
Ran away from what you so wanted
How you're so very haunted
So very haunted

The sign has been out for quite sometime
Myself wanted
The sign has been out for quite sometime
Myself wanted

The daily mask goes on
The daily gloves come off
The daily thoughts float through
The daily hiding of everything soft

The true core is a lie
The progress digresses
The worldly influence
The worldly successes
It's so funny how

You're not so funny now
It's so ironic
You've created your own tonic

How you ran away from what you wanted
Ran away from what you so wanted
How you're so very haunted
So very haunted

The sign has been out for quite sometime
Myself wanted
The sign has been out for quite sometime
Myself wanted

I slowly got healthy. I didn't eat solid food for thirty days after the transplant. I drank too much coffee and I smoked way too much while I was going through all of this, but I never went back to the bottle.

In the winter of 1998, I weighed 130 pounds. Not much for a 6-foot frame.

The mirror revealed a reflection of Jim Morrison in leather pants. Of Jesus on the cross. The only way to romanticize the effects of nine months of chemotherapy and a bone marrow transplant is to create the illusion of being a very cool thin white dude or repeatedly celebrate the fact that you can now fit into the Sergio Valente's jeans you had in junior high.

You try to look like a person when, in fact, you are just a skeleton with casing. Your gums bleed. You shit chicken soup. The only way you can feel your dick is if you catch it in your zipper. You're cold all the time.

You say things you regret or you can't remember saying at all. Your hair. Your hair is gone (yes, all over). You're thin. You're pale.

You look like Uncle Fester if he had spent time in a concentration camp.

This is the price of living. Complete renovation. Gut the house, Steve! We need to lay down hardwood floors.

Man, did I ever have high expectations of life. What ever happened to the suburban dream. A garage, a job with a tie, a kiss, and a wave goodbye. Kids who say aww shucks and a bag full of big bucks.

Someone took the fairy book and threw it in the fire.

Top Ten Amazingly Painful and Humiliating Incidents of Treatment

1. Attendant cutting tops of non-frozen feet with razor to insert tubes for dye test
2. Needle punched through knuckle by rookie blood collector in search of a vein
3. Lines being ripped out of neck and arm multiple times while restrained to hospital bed (I have attachment issues.)
4. Having a feeding tube in—a small chain shoved up your nose, coming out of your mouth
5. Starvation coupled with the inability to swallow and the absence of any desire for food—40 days and 40 nights and no religion named after you
6. Ground Zero (where your body is down to no blood counts)—feels like elephants standing on top of the elephants standing on top of your neck (The unbearable numbness of being)
7. The taste of chemicals at the back of the throat; learning to associate certain colours with taste and toxicity (Not found at Baskin Robbins)
8. Black veins of fire after too much dosage of chemo drug—the feeling that someone flicked a lighter on high inside your arm
9. Constipation—Man you don't know how much not going hurts until you haven't gone for three days; you'd stick a fire hose up your ass and turn it on full blast if it would take the discomfort away
10. Psychosis, being in a different world everyday…complete loss of any placement in reality—you question

your surroundings for months, maybe years after-
wards—am I writing this or is it a illusion? (Look!
Strawberry fields forever and over there Joe Strummer
naked on a surf board)

Honorable Mentions: Being stabbed in stomach for liver
biopsy, wheelchair accidents in malls, and playing golf
with a PICC line in.

Purgatory

Do you remember the night?
I embarrassed us all
I never got close to the mountain
Before I started to fall

If I was ever myself
If I ever was alright
It certainly wasn't that night

Couldn't handle the emotion
Experience the pain
Celebrate the occasion
Handle the shame

If I was ever myself
If I ever was alright
It certainly wasn't that night

Father please forgive me
For what I have done
Father please forgive me
For what I have done
He says no absolution for that one
He says no absolution for that one

I got the message
Wrote it up on the chalkboard
Cleaned out the ashtrays
Praised the lord

It still sticks with me
Though it starts to dissipate
Telling me what to do
Something I fucking hate

If I was ever myself
If I ever was alright
It certainly wasn't that night

Father please forgive me
For what I have done
Father please forgive me
For what I have done
He says no absolution for that one
He says no absolution for that one
Maybe I'm asking the wrong person

15
ABSOLUTION

Since I got myself dried out back in 1995, I was able to clean up my act.

I'd held a full-time job in and around all the illnesses, and I'm proud to say that alcohol hasn't affected my job performance since those faraway days.

Am I ashamed of the way I acted when I was drunk? Of course I am. Do I wish I could change things? Yes, of course I do.

I've committed sins. I've hurt people and I wish I could take a lot of things back, but I can't. I have repented, but at what point are my sins absolved?

When do I become forgiven? When is judgment day?

When I was drunk, I was not a nice person to be around. I lied and I cheated and I stole.

My first wife bore the brunt of my anger. It was never physical, but I said things that she didn't deserve to hear. I don't like to think that the personality I displayed back then still lives in me, but I am well aware that it does. You just have to hook me up to a ventilator and some heavy narcotics to see it. World's worst carnival game.

That seems like another lifetime ago. Between then and now, I'm proud of the man that I've been. I'm proud of how I've maintained a relationship with my daughter and she knows whenever she needs me, I will be there.

The punishment doesn't always fit the crime. I have been paying for crimes that I committed in the George Bush Sr. administration. I have forgiven myself, for the most part. Have I been forgiven? I don't know.

16
ACADEMICS & ADVERTISING

I HAD TO GET a formal education of some kind if I wanted to be successful. If nothing else, I wanted to set an example for my daughter.

A trail of college, university, and training courses followed me around up until this point. It just amounted to a degree in confusion with a major in crazy. I took mostly business courses, but I also dabbled in studying filmmaking and screenwriting.

My friends at the time were mostly taking social work and addiction counsellor courses to work in the field (rehab, addiction services, and case workers), and I thought that would also be a good area for me. I decided to take correspondence courses through McMaster's University and I ended up doing quite well.

I volunteered at a local rehabilitation centre. I went so far as to apply to a new addictions counsellor course at the college in Charlottetown. I was denied admission because I didn't have a degree in anything. That, in hindsight, was a very good thing—after working around the rehab awhile longer, I could see the insanity of the disease and the constant state of denial of the same clients.

I would have become too frustrated at the lack of outcomes. You only draw maps in that business; you can't except people to follow them.

From Bobby

Steve really wanted to go to school to become an addictions counsellor. It's not unusual for addicts to do this. You have an epiphany and you think you can share your brilliant insight to save the world. Steve really wanted to help addicts, until he realized that his job would be sitting and listening to people whine about their lives all day. And that wasn't going to work.

Soon after that local school denied me, I received a phone call to come for an interview with the phone company in Halifax. I was given a job as a channel manager in the new high speed Internet division (broadband). It was about three months after I started that I got sick again. I had wanted to take a diploma in Marketing and International Business. It would have to wait until after the BMT (Bone Morrow Treatment, not the classic Subway Bigger Meatier Tastier sandwich).

I went back to school for that diploma in Marketing and International Business in 1999 and I did so well that my professor told me that I should continue on and get an MBA. Eventually I would.

In 2000, I was promoted to the advertising department of the company I was working for and, within a couple of years (2002), I was promoted again to a higher-level position in marketing strategy.

I met this girl at work. She was beautiful and smart and funny. She worked in HR.

I was having an issue with a customer and it was getting ugly. I told her if she could get this asshole off my back, I'd buy her dinner.

She agreed. And she straightened everything out for me. Thank God. Otherwise, I'd actually have to ask her out on a real date, which normally wasn't an issue for me, but things were different with Sandra because I really liked her.

We started dating in March 2002.

From Sandra

Steve sort of tricked me into going out with him. That's not to say I wouldn't have agreed, otherwise. But that's how it happened.

We'd worked together. I was in the HR department and he needed my help to calm down an irate customer. He told me that if I could straighten out the problem, he would buy me dinner.

Of course, I fixed the issue and Steve held up his end of the bargain.

But when he told me what restaurant he was taking me to, I did a bit of a head tilt. It was one of the nicest restaurants in Halifax. I told my friend/roommate/coworker and she confirmed what I was thinking—that this was actually a date.

Now, Steve had a reputation for being a ladies man, so that friend was a bit worried for me. She told me that if he tried anything that she would come and pick me up.

We had an amazing date. We took my puppy, Gunther, for a walk. Then we went to dinner. After dinner, we went to a movie. Unfortunately, we had to leave before the movie finished because the power went off and we were told we had to evacuate because of a fire across the street.

We went out to Steve's Jeep, which happened to be parked in front of the burning building, so we couldn't get to it.

I ended up having to call my roommate after all.

Steve at age 4

Brothers

Steve at age 7 in Inuvik, NWT

Steve, first day of school, Iverness, Cape Breton

Little "Wayne Gretzky" in Inuvik, NWT

High school graduation

Steve at age 14, Dartmouth, NS

Playing football, Grande Prairie, AB

Sandra's and Steve's wedding, 2004, Baddeck, Cape Breton

Sandra and Steve at home

Kelsey and Dad, 2003, Halifax, NS

Sam, 2014, Stratford, PE

Steve with parents Barb and Don Webster at MBA graduation

Island Life, 2010

17
AND AGAIN

I WAS GETTING RADIATION therapy on my neck at the time—a maintenance thing. Sandra was aware of the fact that I wasn't in perfect physical health, but it didn't matter to her. She even came with me for some AA events and some of my treatments. She brought me home to meet her parents for Easter. It was very serious between us. By July, we were living together.

During our move, I had to go to a doctor's appointment. It was there that I got the news that the cancer had come back. I was starting to lose track.

Through all those years, I had taken the whole cancer thing in stride. This time, though, the fourth time, I was scared.

The cancer had spread and they had exhausted all of the options available to me in Halifax. What the fuck would happen now?

From Sandra

We found out the cancer had come back.

Steve and I were out for a drive in his Jeep, looking at houses. He was particularly quiet on that drive. I knew there was something on his mind.

Eventually, he blurted it out. He told me that he would understand if I wanted to end things. He knew what I was going to be in for and he was trying to give me an out.

He had said it as casually as if he were asking me to decide what I wanted for supper.

I remember telling him he wasn't going to get rid of me that easily and that we were going to get through it together. And we did get through it. We always will. For better or for worse.

If you have cancer, the big question you have to ask yourself is: What are you willing to do to stay alive? How strong is your will? How much can you bear?

Treatment sucks and it's hard, but I believe survival is 90% mental and 10% physical. It's a mental game. You have to keep putting one foot in front of the other, trudging through and having your mind in the game.

I read once that the body will actually create a functional reserve, for example an artery where an artery is blocked. The body will adapt and grow and do miraculous things to survive. Your body will do its part, but you have to do the hoping.

My body is a functional reserve.

I've been around people with the same diagnosis as me and you can look in their eyes and see that they're going to die. I don't know where that comes from, but I guess it's a combination of your environment, your personality, your faith, and all kinds of things.

If you ever spoke to some of my close friends, they'd tell you that I'm a very stubborn person. I really think that stubborn, grumpy, cantankerous people make better survivors. We might not make great patients, but bad patients survive more than passive, patient patients.

Accept that you're sick. Accept the battle. Don't accept a negative outcome.

And then, fight for your life.

Tina

All blonde and scared
Time is not a friend
As time goes bye
The search for hope though
Still dances in your eyes

The house is getting beaten
By the storms that come from inside
You hold on tight
As the winds blow bye

But sometimes the gales are too much
And the night becomes too dark to fight
You haven lost anything
You've become part of the light

The world is a little colder
A smile that can't be replaced
The battle for life
Is fought in a god forsaken place

The house is getting beaten
By the storms that come from inside
You hold on tight
As the winds blow bye

But sometimes the gales are too much
And the night becomes too dark to fight

You haven't lost anything
You've become part of the light
You've haven't lost
You've become part of the light

You never lost, Tina
You've become part of the light
See you in the light

Dr. White

The treatment at NIH was not something we had done here before. I had sent [Steve] to see Dr. Wynham Wilson about a clinical trial, but in the end they treated him with a non-trial combination they were working with.

There was nothing else to offer that was likely to give him a remission.

sometimes you have to give credit where credit is due.
and i'm brilliant.
   like a shape shifter.
   they had me pegged wrong all this time.
   too late. too late. too late.
   he's mine.
   i win.
   "We've exhausted all options."
   music to my ears.
   music to my ears.
   let's dance.

18
ALTERNATIVE TREATMENT

I WAS FULL OF cancer and it looked like it was going to win this time. It was in my blood. It's not the greatest thing to happen to a budding romance.

I had a very good doctor, The Good Doctor White, who basically told me that if I stayed in Nova Scotia, cancer would finally kill me.

I found out about a clinical trial happening in the States. Dr. White got me the contact information for the hospital, and I was accepted into the trial. The trial was happening at the National Institute of Health (NIH) in Bethesda, Maryland. NIH is one of the best medical research hospitals in the United States. Probably the world.

Sandra stayed behind in Halifax to work and Dad came down with me. I was so sick that Dad didn't know if he would be able to get me on the plane. Dr. White told him we had no choice. If he didn't get me on the plane, I would die.

We made it to Bethesda and stayed in a hotel about a block from the hospital.

I was put on an experimental drug that ended up making me very sick. It started shutting down my organs.

It looked pretty grim. I volunteered to leave in an act of nobility. I felt that I was taking up space and that maybe at least I could help save another life if I left.

I ended up staying. And Dr. Wynham Wilson, one of the world's leading authorities in lymphoma just happened to get my case.

We learned that I had been misdiagnosed back in 1989. It was actually not Hodgkin's Disease that I had back then. It was a rare type of non-Hodgkins Lymphoma.

I had been treated for the wrong thing this whole time.

I am not spiteful over that. They simply didn't know back then.

There's also the possibility that it changed over the years from Hodgkins to non-Hodgkins. It didn't matter. It had taken lots of time, research, and technology to figure out that there were over 60 types of lymphomas all with unique traits. It was my job to take the treatment and to fight.

So, I didn't blame anyone. There was nothing that could be done to change it now. But I couldn't help but wonder what might have happened had we known way back when.

What might have been different?

I had T Cell Rich B Cell non-Hodgkin's Lymphoma. That's a long name for blood cancer, but they thought with the right treatment they could clear it.

But that treatment was going to be like a mini bone marrow transplant.

"We will be using R-EPOCH, a chemotherapy regime consisting of etoposide, prednisone, vincristine (Oncovin) and doxorubicin hydrochloride (hydroxydaunorubicin hycrochloride) which may be used in combination with rituximab (R-EPOCH) for the treatment of various aggressive B Cell and T Cell non-Hodgkin Lymphoma. Arrecombinant chimeric murine/human antibody will be directed against the CD20 antigen, hydrophobic trans-membrane protein located on normal pre-B and mature B lymphocytes. Following binding, rituximab triggers a host cytotoxic immune response against CD20-positive cell..."

That's a lot of Latin for: "stuff that will make you very sick to make you well."

Rituximab was made from the spleens of mice, so it could explain my bias towards cheddar to this day.

I was slated to get a second bone marrow transplant, but a nurse practitioner challenged that decision. Said that if it didn't work the first time, would it really work this time?

They decided to use a new protocol. They would use a course of drugs to bring my blood counts down to nothing and then build them back up again.

Dr. Wilson looked the part of genius because he wore bow ties, glasses, and the kind of cool leather shoes that only smart people wear. Most of all, he was kind and encouraging. Words of hope echo through time when you're trying to create more for yourself.

One of the nurses who was assigned to me was named Pia. She was young, smart, and kind. She also didn't take my shit, but more so, she helped me refocus my energy when I would get stuck in my mind, analyzing everything, looking for the angles. She provided a voice of reason for me.

I have laser-like focus when I know what I have to do. We all need clarity and goals.

I was told I would be put into an isolation unit for at least two weeks on a different floor of the NIH. I would be given drugs that would take my blood counts down to almost zero...including my white blood cells—the ones that fight infection. That meant nobody could come in or out because of the risk of me developing an infection being so great.

The average healthy person's white blood cell count would be somewhere between 4,500 and 10,000. Mine were being brought to almost zero. Having your white blood cells brought to such low levels is an extremely strange sensation. You can't move. It feels like there are elephants standing on top of you. You are numb and you can feel your nerves buzzing beneath your skin.

I was in isolation for seventeen days.

Another one of the nurses was named Patience. No, the irony is not lost on me.

I introduced myself as Mr. Impatience.

Patience was from Jamaica. She had that wonderful lilted accent that was soothing with its implied lack of worry. The room itself was about 10×5 and it had a separate washroom.

My parents had bought me a small TV/CD combo that was placed at a small stand at the front of the room. It was my only source of entertainment.

Nurses and doctors had to wear masks when they entered. All things in and out would have to be cleaned, for fear of infection.

All sharp objects had to be kept away from me. All bathroom visits had to be supervised. Any bleeding could cause serious damage.

I made a friend through the door. A recovering addict who came to the hospital for meetings. They thought we would have something in common to talk about.

He wasn't able to come in the room, but he would talk to me through the door. Once, he brought me a gift. A daily book of reflections. I've read it every day since then. It is tattered and torn. Meant more to me than that stranger could ever know.

During the day it was boring. But I would take the days over the nights anytime.

At night, it was like being in a concentration camp.

Surrounded by the worst cases in the cancer ward. Sick prisoners of the NIH, all in their own cells. Me against the world. Time to find that laser-like focus.

The screams would wake me up from sleep. The screams of people bartering with God.

The cries of families realizing the battle had been lost.

The drugs had me in somewhat of a haze, but I knew what was happening.

Patience would come into my room when the screams were so loud that they forced themselves through the wall of my room into my head.

"You will make it Steve," she would whisper in her soothing Jamaican accent. "You have the will. You have the will." She would put her gloved hand on my chest. Whisper in my ear.

Those whispers drove me forward, through the nights.

Sandra came to visit for a couple of weeks. Mom was there for a couple of months. Kevin came down to visit and Debbie, my birth mother, did too.

During the day, visitors would take turns in the room. I would make them put objects in different places. It was the only control I had.

Everything else was in someone else's hands.

Pia would send me pages of *The Onion* newspaper and I would smirk in the way I smirk about the insanity and hypocrisy of our world. I would write a quote of the day on the whiteboard with my blood counts. "Those who say laughter is the best medicine haven't had morphine" was especially popular with the nurses.

Total Zero Day came. After seventeen days in bed watching The Sopranos, white blood cells were down to next to nothing. I felt like I was underneath a great weight and couldn't move. Everything vibrates, but all the particles feel like pins, and the fatigue is so great it feels that you're being pulled to the next world, but you're on pause in the transfer of states.

Our particles are in the air.

The white coats would come and go and everything seemed surreal.

The doctors would tell me things were going well. I'd respond with a weak smile and a half-hearted joke.

From Pia

Steve should have been dead before he ever got to us.

He was a very sick man, but he had a sharp wit. He was terribly sarcastic, but I liked him and he liked me. Even though he put up a tough front, there was a real softness to him. Niceness and a light in him.

We talked about music and books. Movies and TV shows. In different circumstances, we would have been friends.

We used to sling jokes and insults back and forth, too. He told me once that he saw something on TV about a doctor somewhere up north with breast cancer. For some reason, she had to do her own biopsy and the only person around to administer the cancer drugs was a mechanic. He said to me, "See, even a monkey could do your job."

It was a personal challenge of mine to try and make him smile or laugh every single day. I wanted to stop him from being grumpy. He was angry about his situation, but he never complained about it.

He didn't tolerate stupidity or incompetence. He never cut me down because he knew I would let him have it right back, but he made some other nurses cry. There was one little Korean nurse in particular who refused to go back to his room because he was too mean.

I knew it wasn't him. It was just his situation. I am happy he made it. He and Sandra invited me to their wedding and I was so sorry I couldn't be there. I really regret that.

I was released from my isolation cell with a fanny pack full of drugs that would pump for a day and then I would have to go back for a refill. We stayed at a very nice hotel down the road for those six months after my own personal Ground Zero experience. Every two days it was back to the hospital.

I had all of the people closest to me come down for a visit at some point during those months and I was pretty terrible to be around.

They were in a room with a man loaded on drugs and a bad attitude. I hated that little fanny pack, as even in near death I was very fashionable. Trips to the mall to buy brand name clothes were frequent. Even though I was tall, bald, skinny, and had the wear of chemotherapy, I was convinced people stared at my fanny pack.

OZ

The room is made to sedate
To steady the racing heart
To quiet a tangled mind

You think about the end
Will they remember you?
Will you be alone?

Your face it twitches
Your legs they want to roam
You sit on the side of your cot
And click your slippers

There is no place like home
There is no place like home
The place is so plastic
The dolls all breathe through straws
Praying to the creator to see
Whispering to the creator
Why, why, oh why, fucking me

They sit on the benches
In the artificial dome
They all click their slippers and chant

There is no place like home
God almighty take me home

From Kevin

By the time I made it down to visit Steve in Bethesda, he was pretty settled into his hotel room. And the only thing he wanted to do was go somewhere. Anywhere. Mom and Dad took us for a drive through some part of Pennsylvania and we ended up at this high-end mall.

It was pretty tiring for him, so I got a scooter for him and pushed him around a bit. I felt so bad for him that he couldn't even shuffle around a mall for a little while. It was one of those times we all realized just how fragile he was, except Mom and Dad had been living through it—it was fresh to me and it really made an impact.

After we got back to the hotel, I took out a DVD I'd brought with me. It was Robin Williams *Live on Broadway*, put together after all the stupidity in September 2001. It was hilarious and we all laughed so hard I remember that I was crying.

They were tears of laughter and it was also very emotional to see Steve enjoying something so much.

sonuvabitch. i hate those fucking fanny packs and not for the fashionability factor. i had underestimated him. his strength.

i was growing weary. i was fucking tired. i followed him for tens of thousands of miles over 17 years. i'd suffered dozens of cycles of radiation and chemotherapy. i was blasted with fucking mustard gas.

the trip to maryland was probably the end for me. at least for awhile. i had failed, but i'd come so close.

must regain my strength.

while i did that, i thought i'd leave the killing to the cure this time.

i couldn't get him directly, so fuck it. i don't have to do it myself. i've done enough damage already so it seems.

sweet irony.

sweet, sweet irony.

meanwhile i will be here. i will always be here.

waiting

I walk up the front lawn of the hospital. My eyes are fixed straight ahead of me. I have the "hockey player" face on. I have fire inside of me. I look past people. Or through them. I am a ghost not wanting to be seen.

There are four elevators and fifteen floors and forty people waiting. The elevators are the bane of my existence.

We stop at every floor. The fatter the person, the closer the floor, I mumble to myself. Sometimes I say it loud enough to be heard.

"Have another donut."

"Long walk, Slim."

People look at me and think, he's crazy. It's the drugs.

Maybe it was the drugs or the steroids or the fact that I needed to control something. Anything. The world had been spinning for so long. One day a man with a collar got on with Sandra and me, and he could tell I was agitated.

I blurted, "fuck" under my breath as someone got on and got off two floors later. Too lazy to climb a flight or two of stairs. The reverend looked at me and said, "John Mac Leod, Pentecostal Minister," and he extended his hand.

I replied, looking him right in the eye and said, "Steve Webster, Roman Catholic," and I did not reach out my hand.

I get off at the 13th floor. I felt the strange comfort of being with the rest of the cursed, even though sometimes I would ridicule the weak. The old cancer pro knows not their fear.

Treatment was making a difference, and each day it seemed I felt better, though the wear on my body was showing from muscle loss and a general "beat to shit" appearance/vibe.

I was now able to travel back and forth to Halifax in between treatments, and the company I worked for was good enough to let me use their personal jet which certainly aided in getting away from the germ world of modern airports.

I used to get a kick out of the people wondering about who was going to get off this private plane. All the people creeping for celebrities must have been sorely disappointed. Though I did look like a junkie rockstar. I wish...I mean, at least you'd have some control.

When I left the hospital from my final check up there, I felt pretty confident that I was going to be okay.

Dad and I then drove from Maryland to Truro, Nova Scotia. I wanted to be home in time to go to Sandra's cousin's wedding with her. I showed up with a PICC line in my chest, but I played golf with the rest of the guys.

That was the last time I've come face-to-face with Cancer. But it's far from the last time I've come face-to-face with death.

From Don

When we were in Bethesda, at one point, Steve got it into his head that he had to go to the movies. Come hell or high water, he was going to see a show. He couldn't walk a block because he was so sick, so we got a taxi to take us to the theatre.

When the movie was over, we got a cab back to the hospital. We got back to the room and Steve told me that he lost his wallet. Steve is famous for losing his wallet.

I hustled back down to the theatre, but they wouldn't let me in to see if I could find the wallet because the next show had already started. So, I waited until the movie was over. It wasn't there. The cleaning staff hadn't found it either.

We needed identification in order to get back into the hospital, and thank goodness Steve still had his hospital bracelet on—most times he took it off at his first chance—, but I had to call Sandra back in Halifax to get new copies of his driver's license and birth certificate to send them down to us. This was soon after 9/11 so security was pretty tight around the hospital.

She wasn't overly impressed!

From Sandra

Steve came home for a week in June. I was so happy to see him and he was happy to be home. But he was very weak.

He asked me if we could go for a drive to Peggy's Cove. We put the dog in the car and I drove because Steve had so little strength after all the treatments that he could barely stand, let alone drive.

Steve was insistent that I park somewhere without many people around. I figured it was because his immune system wasn't strong and he didn't want to pick up any germs. So, we found a spot where there was nobody in sight.

We went for a walk, the dog pulling and yanking us along.

Then, with the sound of the waves crashing onto the rocks, Steve got down on one knee. He presented me with a $5 ring that he'd bought at the airport gift shop and asked me to be his wife.

I said yes. Then I helped him back up.

no
no
no
no
no
no
no
no
fuuuuuuck noooooo

I beat it again. I hoped, or the last time. I got home to Halifax in August of 2003, and there I was put on a maintenance chemotherapy regime. I drove through the changing leaves, the remains of hurricane Juan, and a once-a-century snow storm to get my treatments over the next few months.

I had my doubts that the nurses knew what they were doing. I may have trust issues. I would call Pia at home to check on the doses.

"I think they're trying to kill me!" I'd whisper to her through the phone. She would laugh and reassure me.

Christmas was pretty special. With Sandra and my daughter, I had everything. As a gift, we promised a trip to Disney World in the spring—a risky promise for someone in my state to have made. But we made the trip to Florida in March.

christmas 2003 was a beautiful picture. steve, sandra, his daughter,and the dog all sitting around the tree.

the young one opened a gift, huge smile of disbelief. really? we're going to disney world? oh i love you! i love you! thank you thank you thank you!

hugs and kisses and i love you toos. heartwarming scene.

i was ready to strike again. with a vengeance.

i knew it wouldn't take much to take him down physically because he still hadn't regained his strength. but this time, i get him mentally too. emotionally. and i'd also take down that pretty girlfriend of his.

two hearts for the price of one! three if you count the young one. oh she adores him too, she does.

i'd almost forgotten how much fun it was to play fuck with steve. he fights so hard. now he would have all that much more to fight for.

you don't find tough ones like steve too often. but even those tough ones aren't barrier proof.

he was in a pretty good place now and i just couldn't have that. happiness and i don't see eye to eye.

he thought he beat me like his father did.

little does he know i was still in there.

go ahead and think you're powerful against me.

go ahead and think you don't need that bottle to beat me.

eight years sober. you think you have it together? it's time to test your will and see what you're really made of.

C.

Soon after we got back from Florida, we were visiting Mom and Dad. I was lying on the couch watching *School of Rock* and I started to shake... tremble... totally out of control.

One of the nurses had told me I would never make it to my eighth cycle of chemo without my body giving out. She was right. I made it through six.

"Are you okay, Steve?"

"You better call an ambulance."

My head still wanted to fight, but my body had finally surrendered.

I remember. And then I choose to forget.

From Barb

In the ambulance, one of the attendants was going through Steve's file.

"I don't believe this! How could one person live through all of this?"

I assured him that it was true.

"He should have a journal or a book written about him," he said.

19
APRIL 2004

I LOOK OUT THE window of the room. It is gray. In the room, it is gray. In the hallway, it is gray. Life sucked out the emergency exit.

Through the windows, I can envision the flesh tearing away from my bones. I feel forsaken by God and family. A modern day leper. Shunned.

So, I listen to the music in my headphones as I walk up and down the hall of the 8th floor cancer ward.

"Driving me Mad" by Neil Finn on repeat.

I am a skeleton with huge green eyes. The drugs, the steroids, pumping through my heart as I walk obsessively up and down the hall with a pole of intravenous in my hand like a Shepard's staff.

"Follow me to Hell on Earth. First come, first served."

Through the haze, some days I feel like I could solve quantum physics. Others, I can't remember where the hat I'm wearing is.

"Welcome to Dumbfuckastan. I will be your guide!"

I recall being a kid, watching *Pride of the Yankees* about Lou Gehrig. I wondered if I would be a martyr as well.

Will they name a disease after me? I have Steve Webster disease. It's terrible. I'm always defensive, aggressive, and critical. Plus, I can't stop saying the wrong things at the wrong time.

Probably will be some type of mental illness, my disease . . .

A bunch of tests had revealed that the chemo had attacked my lungs. I was hooked up to a ventilator where I then got an infection.

Kevin had to be called home from Alberta.

I was given 48 hours to live.

They did a biopsy on my lung and I started to go downhill very quickly.

I wasn't able to breathe.

Another coma.

I lost touch with reality.

I was going to die.

Augustine Cove

I battle for my dignity

All that means something to me
I struggle for security
With all that has been taken from me

Sadness beckons
Waves come more often
Losing it I reckon
Nothing ever softens
The terse black

When the night falls
And it falls
When the darkness calls
And it calls

Water comes and water goes
Inside I feel the tide
The ebb, the flow

I see a window
And a light
I see an old cottage
It seems like a safe harbor
Protect me from the night
Protect me from the night
I stay alone with the beasts

The only one they can feast
Upon in the night
I carry the albatross
For all the love I can't come across
In the night

When the night falls

And it falls
When the darkness calls
And it calls

Time for me is never long enough

I was curled up in the fetal position in a hospital bed. Like a young child listening to music, I started to sing the old Irish song "Carrickfergus."

A handsome rover from town to town.

The room was Clockwork Orange with the furniture moving around like in some cheap 1960s special effects for a Monkeys episode. I was in the in-between world where nothing seems real, yet it all seems too real.

From Dr. White

Steve was critically ill. The worst was the period of time in ICU with pneumonia, which required an open lung biopsy. He was close to not surviving that.

From Sandra

Kevin was called home.

I was scared. I was sitting with Steve in the hospital and he started hyperventilating. He didn't want me to leave. He had never asked me to stay with him in the hospital before.

Steve couldn't breathe on his own. He was hooked up to the ventilator again, for about 7 days. It was one complication after another.

He kept getting worse.

They did a scope to see what was wrong with his lungs.

Don and Barb were staying with us in Halifax while all of this was going on.

I remember walking into the waiting room when Steve was in the ICU after the scope. Barb was there. Her face was gray.

"What's wrong?"

"The doctor said no."

Don was calling Kevin to come home because Steve's organs were shutting down.

From Kevin

I got on the first plane I could. That's what you do when you're told your brother is going to die.

When I got to the hospital, to the ICU, they were extubating Steve.

The first thing he said?

"Fuck."

We all breathed a huge sign of relief.

PART THREE
2010–2014

20
ARISE

I WAS WHEELED OUT of the QE2 a month after coming out of a coma.

Like an animal that had been in a cage, the sunlight and air attacked all my senses. I was used to the staleness of the institution.

I slide into the back of the van; once again with the frame of skeleton. My head, being the heaviest part of my body, wanted to go towards the window. I put a pillow up to hold it still. The whole trip home was a blur.

The weeks to follow would also become a blur. With the drugs in full effect, I was either phoning people to go to the Stanley Cup finals with me at 4am or trying to drive to the coffee shop for a donut, even though I couldn't walk down our front steps.

I would crawl up the stairs of the house to have a bath because I would rather put my hand in a blender than have anyone do something for me. I had to teach myself to live again by going through every little action myself.

Over and over. It helped me get well but it was very hard on my body.

I ended up with a ton of bruises and cuts but by the time the summer was over, but I had gained 20 pounds, could walk up my stairs, and could manipulate a laptop (to surf porn, just kidding).

Brain dominates blood, I would say.

Brain dominates blood, I would say

Say it again.

Get married October.

Back to work after that.

Brain dominates blood.

21
AMORE

IT WAS A pretty special day, mostly because I was marrying the woman I love and am meant to be with, but partly because I wasn't sure I'd live long enough to wear another wedding band. It was a hard year for us, and I found the whole event to be pretty healing.

The ceremony was held in Cape Breton, where my beautiful bride grew up. Her dream was to get married overlooking the Bras d'or Lakes. I was happy to make that dream come true.

More than 200 of our friends and relatives from all over the continent came to the wedding, and most of us were staying at The Inverary Resort, a Celtic/Scottish lodge, overlooking the Lakes. My friends Bobby and Neil were ushers, and Dad was my best man.

We'd originally planned on getting married on the Canada Day long weekend (July 2), but after I almost died in April, we thought it would be best to push the date back a little bit, to October 15.

It looked like it might rain that day. There was a little rain in the morning, but we weren't too worried. There was a tent set up by the lakes that we were going to get married in and the reception and dinner were going to take place in the resort's main hall.

From Sandra

My bridesmaids and me were in the resort spa getting our make up and hair done. We were running a bit late. The ceremony was to start at 4:30 and it was about 3:30 when we were finally getting ready. That's about the time when Don came in.

"Sandra, we have a little problem."

The skies had opened and there was a torrential downpour happening. We wouldn't be able to get married in the tent because it was filling up with water. We had to find an alternative location, suitable for 200 guests. And we had one hour to do it.

The convention centre was already set up for our meal and it would have taken them too long to take it down, set it up for a wedding ceremony, then reset it for dinner.

The staff at the resort was awesome. Because it was the off-season, there was a restaurant/gift shop not being used. They squeezed in chairs, lots of cousins and friends helped out, and it worked out alright because there were windows overlooking the dock and it was quite beautiful.

Seeing Steve look so nervous was sweet.

It wasn't a traditional setting, but we're talking about Steve's wedding. It couldn't be traditional anyway.

And it was perfect.

Sandra's father walked her down the aisle. Past the bar. Through the gift shop and to me.

After we were married, the sun came out.

After photos, we had a great dinner. My daughter welcomed Sandra to the family. I made everyone cry with a pretty emotional speech. But I was emotional. Six months before that day, everyone in that room was told that I didn't have much time left because my organs were shutting down.

The dance went on into the next day. The resort sold out of Alexander Keith's beer, to give an indication of how much fun people were having. We closed the thing down and conked out in the honeymoon suite.

The next morning, I had breakfast with my first sweetheart, my little girl, before she flew back to her mother. We went to Sandra's parents house for a gift opening, and then it was time for my big surprise for my new bride.

A surprise honeymoon to New York City. Wherein we almost got divorced. Note to the betrothed lovers of the world: don't choose to drive to New York City on your honeymoon. Navigating the tunnels and turnpikes among a sea of New Yorkers isn't the most romantic experience. It's probably not the best idea for couples in new relationships to make the voyage from Atlantic Canada to Manhattan. Just putting that out there.

Having survived cancer and New York City together, I think we both felt pretty confident that we could get through just about anything.

22
AWARE

I STARTED BACK TO work full-time in January 2005. I was given a strategy position in a little regarded segment of the company. It would become a very hot department.

I put my head down and worked very hard to turn what was just a thought into a functioning and successful enterprise. I had become somewhat of a favoured son again.

I seemed to have all of my shit together, so I figured the timing was right to apply to the Executive MBA program at St.Mary's University.

I managed to get into that MBA program, I suspect more on character reference then on previous academic achievement.

After all I had been through over the years, you'd think I'd have grown a bit of a tough skin, but I was still scared shitless sitting at my desk in August 2007.

I was sitting among vice presidents and directors of major companies.

It only took a couple of classes before I started to mellow out a bit. I had four other very bright people in my group and I realized that I could hold my own intellectually. I knew if I worked hard, it was going to be all right.

I have always said that "with grace comes responsibility," and I feel I've done my best to give back to other people dealing with, or surviving, cancer.

I served on the boards for the Lymphoma Foundation of Canada and Cancer Care Nova Scotia, and I helped lobby for Rituxan to become approved for treatment in Nova Scotia.

I was nominated to attend, and created policy at, The Live Strong Leadership summit for cancer survivors.

I helped create policy for Adolescent and Young Adult Cancer survivors through the Canadian Partnership Against Cancer, and have spoke on survivorship issues at various conferences.

I've spoken to graduation classes and helped create leadership-training videos for Capital Health's over 10,000 employees.

Most importantly, I have met one-on-one with people and helped them face their life now and, sometimes, their death.

I guess because of my Houdini-like quality of regularly resurrecting myself from the dead, I get phone calls. People with terminal cancer will call me. These people are dying and they think I might have answers. My answer is usually the same. I tell people to advocate for them selves and to research and become well-informed.

Talking to these people when it's too late isn't easy. And honestly, who knows if there was ever a chance to begin with. But one thing I know is true: The greatest of all human emotions is hope.

Hope of a better day. Hope of a better life. Or just the hope of more time with whomever you love.

Dealing with souls who are close to dying and who have died has given me some poignant insight. There are worse things in life than dying. It is important to die with dignity and surrounded by love and to know it is another phase of life.

I was diagnosed so long ago it feels like another lifetime—I guess it was.

In 2007, I started being asked to speak at different conferences around Canada and the US. Sandra came with me to New York a second time (we decided to fly). The conference was happening at a Marriott Hotel in Brooklyn.

During the conference, God played a funny joke on me. Sandra and I were hanging out at the swanky concierge lounge on top of the Marriott with a bunch of other members of the Board of the Lymphoma Research Foundation. One of the people there was the bone marrow transplant specialist in Halifax who was very British and straight-laced. We had always had a personality conflict, but there we were, both speaking at this conference.

I went up to him and apologized to him for basically being me and for challenging him so many times—he'd given me my first bone marrow transplant.

Anyway, it was a neat moment. He told me he always considered me to be an intelligent enough person to make my own decisions. I found that funny, considering our history, and I guess it was true. (There was a Russian intern I encountered on one leg of my medical journey who used to come to me to ask questions about hematology.)

It showed me, once again, we are all just human beings, doing the best we can.

i am weak now, but i will always be with you. even if i don't have my hands gripped around your throat, i'll always be here.

you've thought you had me beat before.

remember?

we know who the fucking boss is around here.

it's not steve webster.

i've owned your ass since the minute you took your first breath and i will be the one who decides when you'll take your last.

directly or indirectly.

for now i must rest.

C.

23
ARTIFICIAL INSEMINATION

First comes love, and then comes marriage. Within a couple of years, it was clear that Sandra wanted to have a baby. I wanted her to be able to have a biological child of her own. I was happy with my daughter and I would have been happy to adopt a child, but I wanted Sandra to have that other option.

When Anne got pregnant with our daughter, the doctors had called it a miracle. I had had enough radiation and chemo treatments that they thought I wouldn't be able to father children.

Back then, my doctors recommended that I store some semen in case I wanted to father a child again one day.

The years went by and I continued to pay the storage fee to the University of Alberta, where the sample was being kept. But eventually I forgot about it and I stopped sending those payments.

I called the storage facility at U of A to see if the sample was still there and, if so, if it was still viable.

The woman on the other end of the phone told me it was funny that I should call because she had come across my sample recently and wondered if I had ended up making it. She was going to call me to see if she should get rid of the sample. Despite not paying the rental fee, the sample was still there and it was still viable.

Our son was born on August 8, 2008.

08-08-08

My second miracle baby. Sam. Simply A Miracle

Considering the age of the sperm, I was relieved that Sandra didn't give birth to a sixteen year old with a mullet and a mustache.

From Kevin

Steve gave me a call one day and he sounded different than he usually does. Steve and I didn't talk daily or even weekly when we weren't in the same postal code. It was just the way we were. But when we did talk, it was usually lengthy, and we got into all kinds of things. We'd talk about sports, politics, and personal matters.

We covered a lot of ground in an hour-long talk. So, it was out of the ordinary for him to be so hesitant about asking me a question on that particular day.

I was starting to get freaked out. I couldn't imagine what he'd be so nervous about asking me. He was wondering if I would help get his sperm from Alberta to Halifax. Oddly enough, the question didn't phase me at all. He told me years before that he had to self-donate sperm because of the cancer treatments he was undergoing. The doctors wanted to ensure that he would have a store in the event that the treatments made him infertile.

I told him I'd call the University of Alberta where the storage facility was to find out if the semen was still viable. But, I wasn't given any information because of protection of privacy legislation so he had to make the call himself.

I remember suggesting to Steve that if they did have a viable sample, he should look into a seat sale to get all those sperm on a plane from Alberta to Nova Scotia.

Anyway, I was very excited for both Steve and Sandra that they were going this route and we all hoped it would turn out for the best (as it did).

My only concern when I talked with him later on, in jest, was that they may have mixed up the samples and he would not get a biological son or daughter. Of course, one look at Sam and we know that is not the case. But it was also an inside joke between us, since it never mattered to us about biology. Our own family is a great example of that.

From Neil (Steve's lifelong friend)

Steve has been my friend, confidant, and inspiration for over 30 years. I've known him in the best of times, the most twisted of times, and the times in between. To talk of all that I know of Steve in a few paragraphs is impossible, but I will try and give some colour to a colourful life.

When I first met him, he was a freckled-faced boy who I played road hockey with. If you see his son, Sam, you see Steve as a boy—a mischievous grin and boundless energy. I think Steve and I were always friends. We lived next door to each other and went to school together—when you're in Grade 5, that's how it happens. Unlike my other friendships, we stayed friends.

We spent every summer from age 10 until we were 20 hanging out at our cottages in PEI. We went to the beach, chased girls, ran from park rangers, had our first experiences with alcohol, and spent way too much time taking ourselves seriously. Steve provided me with soundtrack of my formative years, the Replacements, U2 (before they were mainstream), XTC, and anything else that would label us as alternative. We had a brief hiatus in Heavy Metal, but thankfully we recovered quickly (black leather and jeans in the summer was not a good look). We fought over women, friends, and whether Mike Tyson could beat up Bruce Lee, but we generally held no grudges.

I remember when he was first diagnosed with cancer. It was an unexpected conversation to have with your best friend on a wharf in Covehead harbour. I was too young to realize what it meant. Looking back, we probably treated it too lightly—six months of treatment and then get on with life. We did have some late nights of fear and melo-drama—particularly memorable was the repeated playing of Kate Bush and Pater Gabriel's "Don't Give Up" for 3-4 hours while drinking bad wine.

In our early twenties, I was there when Steve's drinking got worse. At that time, all of our downtime seemed to always involve drinking.

Unfortunately for Steve, the disease would not let him go. It got progressively worse before his wedding and accelerated after. I moved away, we lost track of each other for a couple of years, and then he showed up at my door. He had taken a beating but was recovering; it was probably the first time we had a conversation as adults.

We saw each other in the intervening years. I got updates from his parents and I've been on the phone with the airlines a few times to go back and say "goodbye." Through all these times, I never heard him complain once. There was no feeling sorry for himself and he was always looking toward the future.

At his second wedding, once again everything was going forward, and life continues. His wife Sandra is a perfect match—strong and full of life. The two of them have been through a lot, but they keep going. I marvel at their resilience.

I couldn't finish without mentioning Steve's family. If you want to see where Steve gets his strength and his values, look to his family. His parents are the strongest, most supportive people I have ever met.

I think I have seen all sides of Steve over the years—his temper, his humanity, and his determination. I can't help thinking that all that he went through in his early years gave him the tools he needed to endure all that came later in life. He's as stubborn a man as you will ever meet and that has probably kept him going.

He gives me perspective when life gets stressful and keeps me laughing when we talk. He's the bravest man I know and I can only hope that in 30 years we can sit back, relax, and talk about all the stories I couldn't include above.

24
ABSOLUTELY

AFTER MANY LAUGHS, much self-discovery, a thesis on innovation, and a trip to South America, I walked out into a sunny day in Halifax an MBA graduate. I was proud of myself, damn proud. It was the spring of 2009. The world was my oyster. The oyster I was working in was becoming more and more constricting to me.

Most people, when they graduate with an MBA, see the rungs on the corporate ladder clearer and seek ascension to greater wealth and power. Power has been alluring to me and I think sometimes I had more power than title.

In saying that, I was always chasing titles and I always ended up getting sick.

I was like VP of Survival Affairs by the end of my corporate/government career.

More important than the diploma, we had Sam, and the draw of raising him in a small environment around his grandparents made the decision of what to do next pretty easy.

We were moving back to my home, Prince Edward Island, a small place where I had spent every summer of my youth and where both my adoptive and biological family were from and my parents resided. I wanted quality not quantity.

So, in saying that, I decided to negotiate a deal out of the company I was with and move from Halifax, a market with 350,000 people (plenty of connections), to Charlottetown, a market with 35,000 people (plenty of family).

I figured I could use the severance package to fund my own company. I left in the January of 2010. Steve Webster was going to reinvent social media.

Sandra and I started building our dream home by the ocean, while I started my own consulting firm using my story as a backdrop to speak to, and change, businesses. In retrospect, I probably should have gone to see a doctor while I still had health benefits before doing any negotiating, but hindsight is 20/20.

As an entrepreneur, I had limited success as I built my own brand and was offered a couple of high-paying positions in Halifax to be the Director of Marketing in both the private and public sector. That was wonderful for my ego, but bad for my relationship.

Sandra wanted a smaller life around family, and in my heart, that's what I wanted, too.

During that first year in Charlottetown, I was still doing a bit of travelling. I made a trip to Alberta to visit my daughter, which I would do often because I didn't like having to wait for another summer break for her to come stay with me. Every time I would go anywhere, I'd end up horrendously sick with my lungs filling up with liquid. I seemed to have a constant cold and I was just getting used to living with it, I guess. I figured the way I was feeling was my new normal.

Construction finished on the house in April of 2010. I'd get a few contracts here and there, but I was getting worn out physically and mentally with the stress of building a business, being a new homeowner, and raising a young family.

By November of 2010, I realized I was going to have to suck it up and look for a full-time job, I didn't like having to worry about money and I didn't like being cut off from my social network. I told Sandra that if I didn't find something by March, I was going to have to look for something in Halifax.

If I was going to work for someone, I wanted to be in non-profit or the public sector. To feel that my life had purpose.

I was very fortunate that, because of my connections, reputation, and education, I was able to land a good job pretty quickly. At the end of March, I started a position in strategy with the provincial government. The title allowed me to feel good about what I did and, as a bonus, it provided a salary I could rely on and that we could live on.

But that cough kept getting worse. I'd been running back and forth from the doctor's office getting antibiotics, but I just couldn't shake it.

I coughed the entire first three weeks at my new job. I went to the doctor on the 15th of April. He gave me antibiotics and a Ventolin machine. I stayed in bed for the day on Saturday. That Sunday, I was taken to the hospital.

The last thing I remember is seeing an East Indian doctor and hearing him say, "it's a shame when they're young."

25
APRIL 2011

THIS TIME, DAD took notes...

April 17, 2011–admitted to ICU at Queen Elizabeth Hospital in Charlottetown. Platelets 16–Hemoglobin low–had 3 bags of blood. Temp 36. Blood pressure 89/60–pain in side. Shortness of breath. Oxygen low. Heart rate high. Right lung full. Aggressive pneumonia. Put on ventilator at 4am April 18.

From Sandra

The phone rang at 4 in the morning. It was the hospital.
We have to intubate him and put him on a ventilator.
I called Barb and Don, said I would meet them there.
I got there too late. I couldn't see Steve before he was
hooked up to the ventilator and that really bothered me.
While we were waiting, the doctor came in.
"I hate it when this happens to young people like this."
We had to call Kevin. The next 24 hours were critical.

From Kevin

I didn't know what to do. Do I come home again? Do I wait until the morning?

It turned out they were able to find out what he had and they started treating it.

April 18–Slight improvement but had a bug in blood. Had heart failure, fluid in lung and platelets 18. White cells low.

April 19–Given platelets–has harmophilus influenzae ACDEF (no B) Meds. Piptaz. Heart rate 90 and BP 91/55.

April 20–Advised that mitral valve is leaking. Echogram ok. Heart rate 190. Given morphine–no enlargement of heart. Platelets 14–given whole blood.

April 21–Good night. Taken off blood pressure meds. Looks better–off respirator. On Rocephen Solacorteg.

April 23–No temp. Still fluid on lung. Received radiated platelets. Whole blood. Breathing laboured. Mitral valve causing fluid. In constant care. Heart rate 104 and blood pressure 104/47.

April 24–Good night. Clear thinking. Heart rate 102 and BP 113/66. Lungs showing a little improvement on potassium chloride–solvorette 50 mg. Doctor said he should be on oxygen. Got more fluid off. Ultrasound on left leg. No blood clot.

I really didn't know what had hit me. I thought it was a mere blip on the radar. I had forgotten all about hospitals, what it was like to be a patient. Now they were telling me my heart was all screwed up due to chemotherapy? Had nobody seen this coming? I thought the colds were from a weak immune system. I was just playing hockey a month ago.

My mind reacted as usual to the combination of steroids, morphine, and other drugs. I was a raving lunatic looking for someone to blame for my situation.

I didn't really accept the fact something was wrong with me, I was so set on going back to work and finally leading an idyllic normal life. This would repeat for the next two years, little did I know. The refusal to rest and quit would continue to almost kill me.

So being the intense personality I am (I still don't know how they let me go), I discharged myself then against doctors' orders, after having been in the hospital for roughly ten days.

My doctor didn't know me well enough yet, apparently.

I went back to work. May passed, but then June came along and I realized why that early discharge and return to work was such a bad idea.

We'd had a great weekend at the cottage. We went to see a movie on Sunday. But when we got back home, I knew something was wrong. My heart started beating out of my chest and I was nauseated.

I needed a drive to get some dental work done, so Mom took me to the dentist. I was not feeling well at all by the time I was finished. When Mom started to drive away from the dentist's office, I told her that I thought I needed to go to the hospital. She dropped me off at the door and by the time she parked and came back in, I was being admitted because I'd collapsed in triage.

26
ADENOSINE

Mr. *Webster, we're going to give you a dose of adenosine to stop your heart. It's going to feel like you're being buried alive. That's normal.*

Are you fucking kidding me?

My heart is pounding. It feels like it's going to burst through my rib cage and land on the floor between the nurse and me.

I clutch my chest like holding it will make it hurt less. Like it will keep my heart from beating so hard. Deep, sharp pains. The room is spinning. I think I'm going to throw up. Is this a heart attack?

No, this can't be a heart attack. I'm a cancer kid, not a heart attack victim.

The nurse is ripping my shirt off. Another is coming towards me with a needle. I guess it wasn't the two hours of sleep last night or the nachos I had for lunch making me feel like shit.

Poor Mom must be terrified. Again.

The needle is in. I watch the monitor to see myself flatline. Watch myself die.

Try to relax. What you're feeling is normal.

Normal. What does that even mean?

My eyes are bulging out of their sockets.

I can't fucking breathe!

I try to scream. I try to scream my last words. Sandra, Kelsey, Sam, and Kevin. I love you. Mom, Dad I'm sorry for putting you through this. For dying in the wrong order.

These are the last things to go through my mind as I die. What is this I'm feeling? Bigger than dread. Bigger than fear. Doom.

He rubs the paddles like on TV.

CLEAR!

Black. I'm under water. I pass out. I'm alive, but I'm dead.

27
ASLEEP

Where the fuck am I?
Arms. Tubes. Pull.
Ouch.
Can't breathe. Ventilator.
Sandra?
Blink.
Shuffle thoughts.
Can't breathe.
Fucking ventilator.
Hospital.
Fuck.
Black.
I am awake again. At least I think I'm awake. Need water.
Air.
Get these fucking things off of me.
I rip at the tubes in my skin. Get them off. Get them out.
The nurses barge in.
Steve, you're in the hospital. There's a tube in your throat.
We're going to take that out so you can breathe on your own.

Removing the tube is like someone has opened the door on an airplane before choking you to death.

Get the fuck away from me.

Have to get these things out of my arms.

He's pulling the IV out. Steve, you need to stop that or we're going to have to restrain you again.

Is that really fucking necessary?

We need to restrain you, Mr. Webster.

28
ABLATION

My HEART, IT turns out, was in much worse shape than a mere leak.

The dam was broken and jammed.

I was rushed by ambulance to Halifax, which was 3.5 hr trip from Charlottetown.

I had open-heart surgery on my leaking valve and while they were there the surgeon cleared out my artery which was ¾ blocked.

The next day a stitch broke and they had to open my chest up again to re-sew.

Remember that I have no blood clotting ability to speak of and a suppressed immune system.

I don't really remember the month of June, 2011. Periodically I would jolt back to reality.

I couldn't swallow as they kept shoving vents into my throat. I had lost around 40 pounds. They keep pouring drugs to into me to sedate me.

When I'm under the influence of mood-altering drugs, the worst of me is revealed. The same personality that came to the surface when I was drunk comes out when I'm on those serious drugs they like to pump through me to numb the pain.

Being in a drug-induced coma means living a nightmare you can't wake up from.

Imagine hearing the muffled voices of people talking all around you, but not being able to open your eyes to see them.

"Can he hear us?" they ask.

The weight of a hand on your arm brings comfort, but you have no control over your body to acknowledge the sensation. You drift in and out of different states of awareness, never knowing what's real and what's a dream.

When you sleep, you enter the world of Alice. You go through the looking glass and go on a trip that you can't check out from.

When you're lucid, a member of the hospital's administrative team visits you.

"Steve, do you have everything taken care of? Do you have a will prepared?"

Fuck off. That is none of your business. I'll let you know when I'm ready to go, thanks very much.

Blood is being pumped into you. You hear your name. The beep of the IV pump. The ventilator breathing for you.

You never get used to having a machine breathe for you. It's a slow form of torture. The pace is set to something that's appropriate according to your age and size, but it feels like it's suffocating you.

You have no sense of reality.

Images and sounds merge together to form hellish nightmares. I heard a story once about a man in a drug-induced coma who had vivid dreams of being in a battlefield in Vietnam and being shot over and over in the chest with blood flying everywhere.

When he recovered, he learned that in reality, he'd suffered an arterial bleed in his airway. The doctor who was repairing the bleed was Asian.

I have learned that it's best that I sleep.

Letter from QE2 Hospital

August 2011

Dear Mom,

I write this as if coming out the other side of a big storm
that I was in the middle of and suddenly all is silent and
I can let out a deep breath.

But I remember the storm, the war, and how you dragged
me into this foxhole.

It seemed the air outside the windows was full of the
whirl of helicopters blades and engines in descent.

Was it the drugs creating this image of being in a tower,
held in a room with constant assault from all sides like
some distant war?

I would wake up to moments of clarity and you would
be there, massaging my feet or hands. I had become a
skeleton clinging on to the edge of a ledge.

All the drugs from previous cancer treatments had
played havoc with my heart.

I was 43 with a wife and two children, one three and
one eighteen.

Everything with my heart was broken, it was leaking,
and the rhythm and the main artery were plugged.

I had two open-heart surgeries, three lung infections,
and two comas all in the past month and half.

I haven't seen the outside of this room, save for some
walks down the hallways.

Every day you, Dad, and Sandra were there.

You would go to mass every day, say a novena.

You would bathe my head, wash my feet. Pray for my very soul beside the bed.

You have always had the most amazing faith. Even in the darkest of days you remained calm. I drew strength from this.

I got out that bed, I learned to walk, think, and live again with you there supporting, encouraging, and loving me.

They say the first step to enlightenment is to know that we know nothing.

We don't know why faith works sometimes and not others, except that it is God's will. Faith is an understanding of this, and acceptance and surrender to God's will.

Mom, you have given me the ability to accept things and move on. Which may be one of life's greatest gifts.

Those who think of themselves at least know the real secret to life and thanks to you; I have seen some glimpses of heaven, here on earth with you.

Love Always,

Your Son, Steve

29
AFTERLIFE

PEOPLE OFTEN ASK me "What did you see in your coma or when you were dead?"

I didn't see the white light at the end of the tunnel, yet I don't feel afraid of the afterlife. I've already seen my Heaven. It was the happiest moments of my life on repeat. I have felt the comfortable feeling, that peace.

The heaven I saw is a huge outdoor ice rink. It's the one Kevin and I used to play hockey on in Inuvik. I'm on the ice. A perfect, unscarred version of myself.

Healthy. I can feel my cheeks growing red. Ice cold air filling my lungs. My legs are strong.

There is no pain.

Blades on the ice making that unmistakable sound. Kevin slapping his stick on the ice for me to pass the puck to him. The slap of wooden stick on rubber puck.

Mom and Dad cheering us on.

The soundtrack of my childhood.

My baby girl wrapped in pink. Her perfect little head with its shock of black hair. My little Elvis baby. My nose inhaling as much of her as it can.

My son with a face exactly like my own. That cheesy grin. His first Christmas. Him and Sandra and me eating pancakes for breakfast.

Me and my buddies on the golf course.

The taste of water after exercise.

Good music on the car radio on a summer day with the windows down.

The first kiss.

Sandra coming down the aisle towards me.

Conversation.

Laughing so hard with Kevin and Ward that my stomach hurts.

The trailer before the movie starts.

My daughter's smile.

Sam's look of mischief.

They are all me and I am all them.

The thing I dread about dying is what happens when the lights go out. I can't stand the thought of leaving them while they still need me, before any of us are ready to say goodbye.

***

The wormholes seem to appear to me sometimes— those moments of absolute clarity. These moments are few and far between, but the circumstances become so vivid because I have been here before. I am always looking for signs. I use the same superstitions to guide me—to show me what path I should follow. But my faith should be with the divine.

From Kevin

Thinking back throughout the years, there are two things that strike me about my brother: one is his generosity with his time and possessions; the other is a sense of compassion for people. There is still the average human side that gets irked in traffic and whatnot, but overall he is not judgmental of people. I think he has always had a knack for understanding that things are what they are and everyone's story is different. Steve's view of the world has influenced his friends since it forces them to think, "hmmm...maybe this isn't black and white after all."

30
ALIVE

The first thing I remember clearly after that hospital stint in Halifax was a little red pillow, given to me by the Heart and Stroke Foundation and sponsored by the company I'd once worked for (oh the irony). You had to squeeze it as you lifted yourself up to make sure your stitching didn't come out.

Sandra, Mom and Dad, all my friends would yell at me every time I look like I wanted to get up. "Grab your pillow!"

It was beginning of August 2011. I had basically spent my summer in the hospital.

Once again, I was being wheeled out into the sun and the air, leaving the artificial world behind me.

We had tried to shield Sam and even Kelsey through-out this whole six-month onslaught but I think Kelsey, because of her age, and Sam, because of my absence, knew that something was wrong.

It was more important now then ever to get back to normal—to prove myself.

Brain dominates blood. Brain dominates blood. I would think in my mind.

I had to teach myself again.

To learn to walk, to lift, to think and to sleep at night. I had the template down.

I would go back to work in September, I had to prove myself, support my family.

I was chasing normal.

Walking in the doors to the government office, September, 11, 2001 (more irony), I am sure my co-workers looked at me like I was a ghost.

A ghost in an ill fitting suit who coughed, hacked, and could barely talk.

"I can't go on, I'll go on," is what Sam Beckett said, and it is the truth about life.

So when I think about all battles medical and mental, here are some things I think I know:

Question authority and be your own advocate.

In Western society, we're taught to never question medical authority. They are the experts; you are not. It's not an even relationship, so you have to level the playing field by doing your own research. You control that part of your care.

The thing about cancer is that it makes us all equal. We're all equally mortal. No matter how many letters we have behind our name or how much money we have in our bank account, when it comes to the baseline of human life, we're all equal. It's a hard thing to practice, but my father taught me when I was a kid that you treat the janitor the same way you treat the professor. That means I don't put anyone on pedestals.

That kind of thinking may get you fired, but for me, it meant that I didn't take the doctors' word as Bible and I did my own research. I became my own advocate, and you should do the same, especially if you have cancer.

Acceptance is key.

Accept it, but don't accept you can't control your part, your part.

Always focus on what happens next. What you can do next to make it better. Small actions or big actions.

Educate yourself. (Just enough.)

Educate yourself, but don't educate yourself too much. Use books and reputable sources of information. Google will give you all the hope and fear that you want.

At the end of the day, always look out for yourself, and don't be afraid to question things. Make sure that people are following up when they're supposed to. Things do fall through the cracks. I am, thankfully, living proof of that. You control that as well.

The big answers are rare and even given all that I've been through, I have not found the single solution to why? Or why me? Or why are we here?

I think, though, that it has to do with being part of the collective. Doing our part no matter how big or how small.

All actions are interwoven. So, all my suffering has made me better and the thought that my suffering might lessen the load for others, or inspire some people, gives me hope.

The three things that I believe have helped me survive are faith (acceptance), courage (pain, mental, physical), and hope.

These are principles I learned through the program of AA and people who went out of their way to help a lost and bewildered man nineteen years ago. I have done the best I can to practice these principles in all my affairs.

I can't drink, I am not the highest power on earth (or in my house), and if I do the right things to the best of my ability, my life will get better.

Faith implies a resolute and courageous act of will. It combines the steadfast resolution that one will do everything that one can do within their control and the results come from the divine. You must believe as much as you can that everything happens for a reason, that your suffering has purpose. That in the end you have a purpose to fulfill—not to know but to fulfill.

Courage is knowing that it's going to hurt and doing it anyway. That your mind can take you anywhere and can help you achieve anything.

Courage also involves action and I always would say to myself, *Action cures fear.*

Trying to have integrity in all areas of one's life and the ability to be true to oneself and one's role in the world under all circumstances and trying to stand up for what is right in all situations . . . this is true courage.

Both are easier said than done, but I tried for the most part to stick to these principles. They all got easier with practice (I've had a lot of practice).

Hope is the greatest of all things to me.

Hope is the carrot on the stick, the promise of something better; my hope was to survive to experience life with my family and friends. I have always had hope that things and I will get better.

When I noticed my first gray hair, I shed a tear. But not for the same reason most people cry over getting older. Most people worry about getting old, I worry about not getting old. The closer you are to death, the closer you get to life.

That hair without its pigment was a symbol of aging. It sort of felt the same as when I noticed my first chest hair.

There was a point in my life when I didn't think I'd get the chance to grow old. To look back at a reflection in the mirror that would show wrinkles and bifocals.

Dreams and goals are funny things.

When you're a cancer survivor, you can't help but look at life differently than other people. When you've come back from the other side, time has new meaning.

That gray hair is hope.

Hope that I will walk my daughter down the aisle.

Hope that I will teach my son how to drive.

Hope that I will be there to hold Sandra's hand when we have our first grandchild. I love those gray hairs because I never thought I'd live long enough to see them.

A man dies and appears before St. Peter at the pearly gates of Heaven.

St. Peter looks at the fellow and says, "Before I can let you in, I need you to roll up your sleeves."

The man is puzzled, but does as he is asked.

St. Peter examines the man's arms and asks, "Where are your scars?"

Still confused, the man answers, "I don't have any scars."

With tears in his eyes, St. Peter asks him, "Was nothing worth fighting for?"

**

I am scarred from head to toe.

john wayne, humphrey bogart, patrick swayze. they were tough. but i got them, didn't i?

i'll get you, too. one of these days, you'll let your guard down and i'll win.

i know you're still watching out for me. i can see it the way your mind races every time you have a fever. i might not be in your physical body, but i'm on your mind. never far from your thoughts.

that's satisfying, but you're much too full of hope and contentment for my liking.

i'm busy now, though, so i'll leave you alone for a little while. i get a lot more young ones these days than i did back in the 1980s. i guess i have the depletion of the ozone layer and vanity to thank for some of it. pesticides and cigarettes help keep me busy too.

i'm on your mind.

on your mind.

until next time,

C.

C,

You were a formidable opponent. I'll give you that.

You played dirty and you got in a rabbit punch or two.

You've left me bruised and broken and scarred.

You might have won a round or two, but you didn't win the match.

I don't know if I'll see you again or not, but if I do, don't expect to see any white flags flying.

I won't give up. So take a ticket, and while you're waiting, go fuck yourself. With all due respect.

This space is my mind is not for rent anymore.

S.

One

Chaos and sparks chewing me up inside
Trying to cast out lightning in front of the monument
Throw in some firecrackers to stir it up
Realize my path should have been narrow
Rather than wide

The bar I set was so high
To measure the wrong things

Almost let life go bye
Almost bought in all along

Then it hit me
Cadence is a hymn
And you are the song
And you are the song

None of it doesn't connect
Even when I went and changed sides
Stuck in bathrooms, I should have never been in
Everything seems to vibrate
Seems like opportunity, a prospect

It stuck with me
Cadence is a hymn
And you are the song
And you are the song

All along, you were your song, all along

So you stop living inward and turned it around
Stop trying to survive and move along

Because all the time you were the one
Who wasn't singing his own song...
Move along

NOT THE END

Made in the USA
Charleston, SC
17 September 2014